Spiritual Tales

Inspired by Spirit

Carmen F. Cordo

DEDICATION

Special Thanks to:

All Spirits of Light who have inspired me all my life. Also, my Father for believing in me, being my number one fan and giving me moral support. Love you, Dad.

Table of Contents

INTRODUCTION

Like many times before, I got into the tub to take a nice hot bath. I sat down and closed my eyes. I felt the tension of my muscles melting away. Complete relaxation settled in. It was a moment when everything stood still. I began to see, in my mind's eye, the image of a male entity approaching me. I had seen the image before during meditation. The image was dressed in a long white robe with a hood concealing his face. He began to transmit his thoughts to me. He was instructing me to create a website. Immediately, I opened my eyes and sat up. "Me, create a website? This is absolutely crazy! I don't know anything about creating a website," I thought to myself.

At first, I wondered if it was to display some of my paintings. Since childhood, I have always enjoyed painting but on an amateur level. I disregarded the idea since I only had a few paintings and viewed my skills as mediocre.

The same message resurfaced a few days later. I ignored it and focused on other things. However, the thought would not disappear.

One day I received a phone call from a relative. Although I had no intentions of relating the story of the website, I felt as if some invisible force were directing me into doing so. I began sharing the idea of setting up a website, but I omitted the part of how the idea manifested itself because she was not a true believer of visions or entities.

"I'm not sure how or when, but I am thinking of getting a website to display some of my paintings. Although I don't have many paintings, I think it would be a nice thing to do," I stated.

She mentioned the name of a co-worker. "He is the perfect person for the job. He is a website designer and very good. Here is his telephone number," she said.

A day later, I was on the phone discussing web design with the person she recommended. A date was set to meet face to face to discuss the details of the project.

The young man was very nice and informative. He seemed to be adept in the field of web design. We agreed on a price, and the project was on its way to becoming a reality. Weeks passed without any word from the person. I decided to call him. He said that his current job demands had increased and he would not be able to undertake the task of creating my website. I remained silent for a minute or two. I could not believe I was back at the beginning- clueless on what to do.

"Hello, are you still there?" he said.

"Yes, I am here. I just did not expect this news," I responded.

Before ending the call, he said, " I am so sorry."

After exploring different options in my head, I decided to look up "how to create a website" online. I clicked and waited until the results appeared. I clicked on the first one. It was about a woman who created a website through a company called SBI. I clicked on their ad and was directed to the SBI site. After reading the introduction, I decided to take a chance and become a member. The program was quite intense and

challenging. It felt as if I were back in school. After many trials and errors, I began to see some improvements. I was on my way to creating a presentable website.

When the preliminary work was done and I was getting ready to add my artwork, I was abruptly steered into another path. The more I attempted to create a page for my artwork, the more dissatisfied I became. It was not working out. Something was amiss.

During a meditation session, I was told that the website was not only for displaying my artwork, but also for spiritual stories. After overcoming the dilemma of developing a website, I was faced with two new problems: I was not a writer and knew nothing about spiritual stories.

As time proceeded, spiritual stories began to manifest. Stories began popping up in my head during my meditation sessions. When I would close my eyes, a movie like image would appear. I would then open my eyes and write the details of what I had seen. In time, I had a number of stories with an assortment of paintings. Amazingly, my painting abilities improved tenfold.

After a while, I understood why it did not work out with the website designer. It was a journey that I needed to do solo. It was part of my life lesson. I needed to explore my inner potentials and grow mentally as well as spiritually. It was the beginning of a new me.

As I continued to listen to the voices of spirits of light and heed to their advice, my connection to the spirit world became stronger and meaningful. With their assistance, I went from being doubtful to confident. Spirits had become my teachers showing me a world of many possibilities.

Life is a complete mystery. When you think you have reached the end of the road, another path appears leading you to a new adventure.

This book consists of some of the stories inspired by spirits.

CHAPTER 1

NEGATIVITY- A LOVE STORY

It was mid-morning and a fresh morning breeze had just arrived, scenting the air with a sweet, calming fragrance. Once again, it was a glorious day in the kingdom of God. Faith, Hope, and Charity were saying their farewells to their younger sister, Negativity. They were on their way to perform a charitable mission in one of the lower realms. Their services were required for the restoration of newly arrived souls.

"Take care of yourself and the house. We will be back as soon as possible," Faith said. Negativity, who was the youngest, agreed to stay behind to attend to the household duties. It was not the first time she had stayed alone in the house.

The sisters were God's perfect creation. They were kind, humble, loving, and loyal to God. They were pristine beings that dedicated themselves to carrying out good deeds.

Negativity was a young girl of remarkable beauty with impressive deep brown eyes, long curly locks, and a slender girlish figure. She was the most innocent and pure of all. Her exposure to worldly matters was limited. However, that was about to change soon.

The following day, Negativity was performing one of her favorite chores: attending to the flowers. It was a beautiful and splendid day; a flowery scent was wafting in the air. She had always felt much comfort and joy when flowers surrounded her. She believed that the fragrance and loveliness of the flowers made everything more beautiful. Life without flowers was like a world without color.

As she lovingly labored in the garden, a stranger was admiring her from afar. Her immense beauty dazzled him. "She is truly beautiful…a flower among flowers," he thought to himself. He approached her, not being able to resist the temptation to speak to her.

So absorbed was she in her gardening that she was unaware of the stranger standing close to her.

"Excuse me," the stranger spoke.

Negativity was startled by the sudden appearance of the stranger. She turned her head around and gazed at him.

"Hello. I am so sorry to disturb you. I hope you don't mind, but I needed to say hello. My name is Lucifer, and I am a soldier in God's army," he said politely. After a brief pause, he continued. "Forgive me for saying this but you are a flower among the flowers. In fact, you are the most beautiful flower in the entire garden," the stranger said.

Negativity was momentarily speechless. After a minute or two, she regained her composure and shyly responded, "Oh, no. You are not disturbing me. I was just attending to the flowers. Hello, my name is Negativity and thank you for the compliment."

Lucifer excused himself after a brief exchange of pleasantries.

Before leaving, he asked, "Is it possible to see you tomorrow morning?"

Flustered by a wide range of never before experienced emotions, Negativity lowered her gaze and softly said, "Yes."

"Well, until tomorrow. I will be counting the hours," he said, with a smile upon his face.

Negativity's eyes remained fixed on the stranger. When he was no longer visible, she rushed inside the house.

Alone, with no one to share the details of the encounter or her feelings, she replayed the event repeatedly. She began experiencing a strange tingling sensation all over her body. Just thinking of him created a feeling of euphoria.

"What is happening to me? I have never felt this way before," she said to herself. She had met the most handsome and fascinating man, and could not stop thinking of him. That night she did not sleep. Her thoughts traveled to the earlier event and upcoming meeting. She anxiously waited for their next encounter.

The following day, Negativity got up early and headed to the place where they first met. She was excited as well as nervous. She was surprised that he was already waiting for her. A surge of adrenaline began spreading through her body. Her heart started beating faster. Upon seeing her, Lucifer got up quickly from where he was sitting.

"Good day," he said.

Lucifer was tall with a muscular physique. His beautiful mesmerizing eyes and child-like smile enthralled Negativity. "He is truly a handsome man," she thought to herself.

After a brief pause, she responded. "Good day."

Lucifer sensed her shyness and proceeded to talk about himself. Eventually, she began to open up. They started sharing bits and pieces of their lives. He made her feel at ease.

Negativity told her sisters about her encounter with Lucifer upon their arrival. They were surprised but joyful at the fact that their younger sister had made a new friend. After meeting Lucifer, the sisters were captivated by his charisma and welcomed him into their home.

For several months, Lucifer and Negativity met and talked for hours. When they were together, time was irrelevant. They were like carefree children enjoying each other's company. They immediately fell in love and began talking of marriage.

"Negativity, will you be my wife?" Lucifer asked.

"Yes," she replied, with tears in her eyes.

"Why are you crying, my love?"

"I feel I am blessed. I am so happy," Negativity responded.

Lucifer gently wiped away the tears from her face. Tenderly, he held her close and said, "Don't cry, Negativity. I promise to love and protect you forever."

Negativity was eager to share the good news with her sisters, but Lucifer thought it was best to wait until his return. He had received orders to return to duty as soon as possible. He promised to return and make her his wife.

"Upon my return, we will set a date for our union," he said in a comforting way.

On the day of his departure, Negativity experienced immense sadness and a profound inner void. She felt as if a part of her had died. It was a sensation she had never encountered before. In order to quiet her mental anguish, she went to her garden, sat among the flowers and reflected on her upcoming wedding.

Weeks turned into months, and months turned into years, and there was still no word from Lucifer. Negativity waited faithfully for his return. She firmly believed he would return one day and keep his promise.

Then, one day, a traveler stopped at the sisters' house asking for water. He had been traveling for days and decided to rest before continuing. The sisters welcomed the stranger and offered him food and drink. Enjoying the sisters' hospitality, the stranger began sharing news of the kingdom.

"Although it took a while for the kingdom to recover after the rebellion, things are now back to normal," the stranger said.

"What rebellion?" asked one of the sisters.

"You didn't hear about the rebellion that took place a couple of years ago? I guess since you are so far removed from the center of the kingdom, it is difficult to keep up with what is happening," he responded.

Eager to hear more, they remained silent and allowed the stranger to continue.

"There was a revolt in the kingdom. A group of soldiers tried to take it over by force, but their plan failed. They were defeated and exiled to a distant planet. I believe the leader of the group was called Lucifer, a high-ranking officer in God's army."

Upon hearing his name, Negativity's eyes widened as the color drained from her face. Immediately, she became disoriented. Everything around her had stopped to exist. Some of her senses had shut down. She could not hear, speak, see, feel or think. She was mentally and physically incapacitated. It was as if all her vital signs had temporarily ceased functioning. Her legs started shaking as a mist of darkness had taken over her vision. Slowly, she began falling to the floor losing consciousness instantly.

When she regained her senses, her sisters as well as the stranger surrounded her. They were trying to comfort her.

"Negativity, can you hear me?" asked Faith, in a worried tone.

Dazed, Negativity looked around and then at Faith. After a brief pause, she spoke, as tears rolled down her face, "Tell me, it is not true…not Lucifer…no, no, no!"

"Negativity, what is wrong? Please, don't cry. There must be a mistake. Lucifer is not capable of committing such an act. He is a kind and gentle being," Faith stated, in an attempt to console her. With the assistance of the stranger, the sisters moved Negativity to her bed.

Negativity continued weeping. The sisters' further efforts to calm Negativity were futile. Perplexed by Negativity's reaction, the stranger apologized. "I hope that my words were not the cause of your sister's sudden illness," he said.

"Of course not! My sister gets extremely emotional when she hears disheartening news. She is a very compassionate and sensitive being. As I said before, we do know a Lucifer. However, I don't think he is the one you talked about," Faith said, trying to appease the stranger.

The stranger remained a short while and then departed. On his way out, he said, "Thank you for your hospitality. I hope your sister gets well. Farewell."

For days, Negativity remained locked away in her room, in total darkness, refusing to eat, drink, bathe or communicate with her sisters. She stayed in her bed with no motivation to get up. Her only thoughts were on Lucifer. The rays of the sun or the fragrance of flowers no longer graced her room.

The sisters were perplexed by the constant sobbing sound coming from Negativity's room. "Why was she so highly affected by Lucifer's unfortunate situation, if in fact it was him?" they wondered. They were not aware of the eternal bond Negativity and Lucifer had created.

After a while, the sisters noticed a drastic change in Negativity. She was unrecognizable becoming gloomy and vile. The majority of the time, she remained locked in her room, avoiding all verbal interactions with her sisters. Even her love for flowers ceased. Every time the sisters approached her, she would verbally attack them. "Leave me alone…I want to be left alone," she screamed. They had never witnessed such behavior from Negativity in the past. The soft spoken, loving and angelic being no longer existed.

One day, while working on their garden, Faith, Hope and Charity heard a faraway sound. It was the sound of pain-filled weeping. "Where is that sound coming from?" they pondered.

The sound increased in force over the following days. They discovered that the sounds were the cries coming from the inhabitants of a relatively new planet called Earth. The suffering of others saddened the sisters. They decided to request permission to go to Earth and assist the needy. Their appeal was granted immediately.

Excited about their new task, they agreed to include Negativity. They felt it was the perfect solution to help get her out of her present mindset.

Faith gently knocked on her door and said, "Negativity, we have great news. We have been assigned to do charity work in a new planet called Earth. We want you to join us. It will be good for you."

Negativity became frantic: yelling and pacing back and forth like a wild animal in a cage. "How dare you include me in your plans. I don't care about your ridiculous charity work. I told you several times that I wanted to be left alone. For the last time, leave me alone!" she exclaimed. Negativity's behavior was getting worst. She was out of control.

Later that day, a thought entered Negativity's mind. What her sisters were offering her was the opportunity she was waiting for. It was the perfect chance to search for Lucifer. Although she did not know where he was exiled to, Earth would be a good place to start.

As the sisters talked about Negativity's behavior and the various options available to assist her, they were interrupted by a noise. It was the creaking sound of a door opening; it was coming from Negativity's room. Negativity appeared looking disheveled, pale and frail. She had stepped out of the darkness and into the light.

The sisters were amazed and overjoyed to see Negativity standing in front of them. Their faces beamed with ecstatic delight as joyful tears ran down their faces. It had been a long time since they were all together. The sisters embraced Negativity and welcomed her back.

"We missed you so much," Hope uttered.

Negativity hugged her sisters and asked for forgiveness. "Please, forgive me for my distasteful behavior. I don't know what came over me. I was not myself. I know you want the best for me. Yes, I accept your offer. I, too, believe that it will help me to overcome what I am going through. Thank you," she stated meekly.

The sisters evaded asking her questions as to why the news of Lucifer had affected her so greatly. They were pleased to have her back to her old self and did not want her to regress to her recent adverse behavior.

Although Negativity presented herself as being very cordial and concerned with the well-being of others, it was a complete fallacy. Her only mission was to find Lucifer.

Upon their arrival to Earth, Faith, Hope, and Charity were

disheartened by the conditions they witnessed. The suffering they observed was on a greater scale. It ranged from slavery to butchering human beings. Humans were divided into two categories: the oppressed and the oppressor. The oppressed suffered afflictions beyond words, while the oppressors remained unsympathetic to the anguish of their captives. The oppressors were empty souls who worshipped the Gods of riches. While some humans cried out to God for help, others simply lost all faith and hope. Although the job was massive, Faith, Hope, and Charity felt optimistic.

Meanwhile, Negativity was secretly devising a plan that would set her free to search for Lucifer.

"I was thinking, due to the magnitude of this job, perhaps it would be best for us to divide and go separate ways in order to assist as many people as possible. There are so many people in need. If we spread out, we can reach more people," Negativity suggested.

At first, Faith, Hope, and Charity disagreed, but after examining the enormity of their mission, they realized that Negativity was right. There were too many humans in need of their help. By going in different directions, they would be able to cover more territory and help more people. Her plan had worked.

They agreed to meet after a certain time. They hugged each other and departed going their separate ways.

Negativity was free to commence her search. She trekked around the globe, and yet she was untouched by all of the misery and suffering that she witnessed. Her thoughts were on finding the man she loved. Days turned into weeks, and weeks turned into months, and still no sign of Lucifer. Nevertheless, she continued to search.

"Am I wrong? Perhaps, Earth is not the place where he was exiled. Where is he?" But her heart affirmed that he was near.

As she journeyed on a secluded road in an unknown region, she heard a voice calling her name. She turned around, but saw no one. She heard the voice calling her name again. Once again, she turned around. This time, a man wearing a dark, long cloak with a hood over his head was standing behind her.

She wondered how he knew her name. "He must be a friend of Lucifer," she thought. "Excuse me, do you know Lucifer?" she asked.

The stranger remained silent.

"Please, can you help me? You must know who he is. You called my name. He must have mentioned my name to you," she said in a desperate tone.

The stranger continued to remain silent. He was admiring her beauty. Disappointed with the man's non-response, she turned around and started to walk away.

"You are more beautiful now than before. Don't you recognize me anymore? How quickly you have forgotten me."

Negativity's heart started pounding and a chill had taken over her entire body. She recognized the voice. She turned swiftly to face him. "Is it really you, Lucifer?" she asked, her voice trembling.

"Yes, it is me," he replied.

Overcome by indefinable joy, Negativity, with tears in her eyes, embraced him. Her search was finally over.

Lucifer had greatly missed her. Although much time had passed, he had never stopped loving her.

After caressing each other for what appeared to be an infinite amount of time, they moved to a secluded area where they sat and talked. It felt like old times.

Lucifer had changed tremendously. He was extremely thin, with a ghostly pallor. Although his eyes were still mesmerizing, they possessed a quality of redness and intense anger. His once beautiful child-like smile was no longer visible.

"What have they done to you?" she asked.

Lucifer replied, "It has been a harsh journey. But your beauty has dissipated all thoughts of the harshness that I have endured. I never thought I would see your beautiful face again. You have brought much joy into an empty heart." Lucifer apologized for not keeping his promise to her. He was unable to return and make her his wife.

"Lucifer, I waited faithfully for your return, but you never showed up. A traveler told us about a revolt in the kingdom and mentioned your name as the leader of the rebels. Please, tell me what happened," Negativity said.

[15]

Lucifer began rendering the facts of his downfall with bitterness. "For some time, I had not been pleased with the way God was handling matters of the kingdom. I was on sabbatical when we met. I needed time to reflect on all that was going on. However, when I met you all of my feelings of disappointment and anger vanished. It was upon my return to duty that the feeling once again resurfaced."

For a brief moment, Lucifer lowered his head and paused. Memories of the past had emerged, causing a brief flow of sadness and hurt. With an intense look in his eyes, he continued,

"Once, I was one of God's favorite sons. He sought my counsel on many issues of the kingdom. He valued my opinion. I was obedient and loyal. No other son could have loved Him more. He was everything to me. I tried to please Him in every way I could. But as time went on and other realms were created, God's attentions were focused elsewhere. I, as well as others, was slowly being forgotten. I was no longer the son He listened to or shared His time with. I was pushed aside. My disillusionment began to grow. One day, God ordered me to intervene in the affairs of another realm. For the first time, I refused and challenged God's directives. He no longer valued my opinion; he just wanted a submissive soldier. When I told Him that our kingdom needed His attention more and not the inhabitants of other realms, He was not pleased and ordered me removed from all military affairs. In an effort to collect my thoughts, I began roaming around the kingdom. I was desperately looking for something or someone to alleviate my inner pain and anguish. Then, I met you. You were like a breath of fresh air. Your presence extinguished the fire that was burning inside me. Our time together was the happiest I ever experienced.

"Then, I received orders of my reinstatement and directed to return immediately. Upon my return, I noticed that things had not changed. My disenchantment grew to a higher scale. In secret, I began gathering some loyal soldiers and formulated a plan to overtake the throne. It took a while before the plan was put into action. When everything was ready, we attacked. Everything was going well until a close friend betrayed me. His name was Michael- the traitor.

"I never thought Michael would pick up a sword and fight against me. We were like brothers. We grew up together.

"During the battle, my soldiers fought bravely and fearlessly, but we were outnumbered. Michael captured and brought me here to this desolated place. My comrades were sent elsewhere.

"When I arrived here, this planet was dark and barren. No form of life existed. I wandered aimlessly in the darkness for what appeared to be an eternity. Although I was trapped in this vile planet, the memory of your love and my immense desire for revenge against God kept me going.

[17]

"Then, from the darkness came a light. Out of the light a figure appeared. It was God. I presumed He came down from the heavens to take great pleasure in seeing my present condition.

"He spoke, 'My son, why have you turned against your father? I have loved you always. It pains me to see you this way.' Then, He paused.

"I assumed He was waiting for me to weep and ask for forgiveness. Instead, with every word He spoke, I felt a burning sensation of rage growing inside of me. Dominated by angry thoughts, I refused to listen to Him anymore. The mere sight of Him infuriated me. Without disguising my ire and disdain, I began verbally lashing out at Him.

'How dare you call me son! Is this how a father treats a son? I served you well and obeyed every one of your commands. You demanded obedience and I gave it to you unconditionally. But when you turned your back on those who loved and served you, I stopped being your son. You don't love. You command. I did what I did and have no regrets. If I had the opportunity to do it again, I would. I despise you and everything you stand for.'

"My son, stop this foolishness and come home," He said.

"I am no longer your son, and you are not my father. I am loyal to no one," I exclaimed.

"God gazed at me as I spoke. A tear ran down his face. By now, I had snapped, and continued to unleash a more violent tirade.

'Please save your tears for someone else. I am not moved. Now, get out of here and leave me alone in this dark and isolated prison you have so lovingly provided for me.'

"God shook His head as if disappointed and said, 'So be it, my son. I will be waiting for your return, for you are always welcome in my kingdom. Meanwhile, this will be your kingdom. Enjoy it!' He turned around and disappeared.

"Time passed and everything remained the same. Occasionally, entities of light from other realms appeared. They called themselves spiritual rescuers. Their goal was to rescue me from the darkness and convince me to ask for forgiveness.

"With hypocritical smiles, they would approach me and say, 'Brother, let us help you to enter the kingdom of God. Ask God to forgive you. He is merciful and compassionate. Come out of the darkness and enter the light.'

"Snarling like a wild animal, I would yell, 'Get away from me you wretched fools before I rip you apart. I am Lucifer. I kneel to no one.' In time, they stopped coming."

Negativity, who had been listening attentively, reached out and touched his hand. It was her attempt to comfort him as he continued.

"Then, one day, a light appeared illuminating the planet. There was light everywhere. It was coming from a planet nearby. When I looked around, I found no sign of life anywhere. My domain, or as God stated 'my kingdom,' consisted of me. When the light disappeared, darkness would return and vice versa.

"After a while, things began to evolve. During the light period, water began to emerge creating bodies of water, and lush vegetation began to sprout bringing forth an assortment of fruit trees and much more. It was as if a painter were creating a picturesque scene using rich, vibrant colors. Soon, living creatures began materializing. They moved freely along the planet while others flew above. At first, I thought it was one of God's tricks to win me over, but I remained adamant in my convictions. My inner hate and hunger for revenge were unfaltering. Hate and revenge were my constant companions.

"One day, unexpectedly, I came across an extraordinary ability. While staring at one of the creatures, and wondering how it felt to be one of them, I immediately felt my body transforming into a replica of the creature. At first, I did not know what was happening to me. When I closed my eyes and formed an image of my former self, I started transforming back to my original form. It was amazing. I began testing my new ability until I became proficient at it. There was nothing on the planet that I could not transform into. I also developed the ability to communicate telepathically. Thought was my biggest weapon.

"While testing one of my newly discovered skills, I transformed into a four-legged animal. I began mentally transmitting my thoughts to a near-by creature. 'Come here...closer,' I kept repeating. When the creature approached me, I viciously attacked it, ripping the skin from its leg. There was blood all around. Hurt and confused, the wounded creature ran away. At that point, I knew I had the perfect weapon to use against God. Since it was impossible to attack God directly, I would use my new skills to destroy all that He created and loved."

Negativity was completely engrossed in Lucifer's tragic story. Occasionally, a tear would glide down her face.

"Then, something surprisingly occurred. I heard the sound of movement. It was not the sound of creatures roaming the planet. It was a distinct sound. Upon investigating, I saw a being taking form. It was in the same likeness of God. Within minutes, another being began materializing. They were different from each other. One was like me and the other one was petite and slender like you. When the process was over, God had created two souls in his likeness and placed them in bodies of flesh. Then, I heard the voice of God. He was conveying a message to them. 'Enjoy all that is around you. However, you must not take fruit from this tree.' The moment I had waited for. It was the perfect opportunity to commence my revenge campaign against God and destroy what He had so lovingly created.

"Taking advantage of the occasion, I transformed into a serpent, planted myself on top of the forbidden tree and waited. In no time, the feminine-looking being appeared. She moved towards the tree and stared at it. I made a hissing sound. She looked up and noticed me on the top of the tree. I slithered down the tree until I was close enough to transmit my thoughts. I said, 'God has sent me down to tell you that He has given you permission to eat from the forbidden tree. It is okay to take fruit. Take and enjoy.' Naïve and innocent, she moved closer. Again, I transmitted the message. 'Take, for God has given you permission.' She looked at me and then at the fruit. Slowly, her hand moved towards the fruit. 'Take it. It's okay,' I insisted. Finally, she grabbed the fruit, pulled it from the branch, and took a bite.

"With the fruit in her hand, she rushed to her counterpart and revealed what she had done. Stretching her hand out to give him the fruit, he shook his head, indicating no. Showing him that it was okay, she took another bite. Noticing that nothing occurred, he took a bite and then another. Shortly, they felt drowsy. Resting on the ground, they closed their eyes and fell asleep.

"A cold breeze awakened them. When they woke up, everything around them was dark and dreary. The forbidden tree had dried up. The paradise God created for them was now a deplorable scene with darkness and chaos all over. They could not comprehend what was happening.

"Suddenly, the voice of God was heard. 'You have disobeyed me. And for that you will no longer be able to stay here. You are banished from here.'

"The breeze had turned into a fierce bitter freezing cold wind causing trees to be uprooted. There was debris everywhere. As the wind continued to gain momentum, they were forced to shield their naked bodies with leafy covering and take shelter behind a nearby tree. The freezing cold penetrated their partial nude bodies causing them to shiver. Not sustaining the freezing cold, they set out to find a more suitable hideout. They were confused and terrified. In an attempt to escape the dreadful cold wind, they walked endlessly. Their feet were swollen and bloody; and their bellies ached. They never experienced cold, pain or hunger. I relished every moment.

"Finally, they reached a desolated dry strip of land. The cold wind and darkness were replaced by scorching heat and light. The place where they once lived had vanished forever.

"They instantly realized that things were different. They could no longer enjoy the beauty and sustenance that paradise provided. In order to survive, they needed to cultivate the land and acquire hunting skills. Life was not easy.

"They began exploring their bodies and soon discovered the method to reproduce. In time, the female's middle part of the body began to grow and soon a male was born. Soon afterward, another one came. I was determined to turn these innocent beings into my instruments of destruction. I would utilize them to destroy God's concept of love. I selected the first-born and began molding the instrument to my liking. I communicated my thoughts, via mind-control, and made them seem as if they were his. I was relentless. In no time, my well-devised plan was being materialized. My instrument had developed feelings of hatred and envy towards his brother. Finally, my plan needed to be implemented.

"It was midday when the younger brother decided to take a nap. While the brother slept, I began working on the older brother. I conveyed the thought to crush the skull of his brother. At first, he hesitated and walked away. I insisted and continued transmitting the message. Suddenly, he picked up a rock and began pummeling his brother's head. I encouraged him with my thoughts to continue. 'Hit him more. Don't stop!' I said, with much excitement. He continued to bash the skull until it was wide open and the face was unrecognizable. Blood began gushing out of his brother's head, ears, nose and mouth. One of the eyeballs fell out of its socket. It was a bloody mess.

"When he stopped, his heart was racing and hands were trembling. He kept staring at his bloody hands. His eyes were wide opened as if in disbelief. Tears began pouring out of him. Petrified by his actions, he ran away.

"I was inwardly happy with the results. My plan was perfectly executed. I had successfully developed the precise weapon to use against God. I called it mind control.

"In time, the feminine creature gave birth to additional sons and daughters. And, they produced other offspring. Before long, the number of these creatures had multiplied. I worked diligently implanting in their hearts and minds the thoughts of envy, jealousy, hate and superiority. Although some were unyielding and faithful to God, many were easily persuaded to walk on the dark side. I created division among them. Shortly, diverse tribes were formed. Each one thinking they were superior to the others.

"At one point, I crafted my own paradise. It was called Sodom and Gomorrah- one of my best creations. In this place, people freely indulged in all forms of depraved acts. Here, God was a meaningless myth. Meanwhile, God couldn't tolerate that His beloved creatures preferred me instead of Him. He became jealous and gave the order to obliterate Sodom and Gomorrah. Massive balls of fire began coming down from the heavens eradicating everything on site. The area was destroyed instantly. Only particles of dust remained floating in the air.

"At that point, I realized how big of a threat I had become to God. He was no longer dealing with a submissive soldier. He was facing divine greatness. I had become a god. I was now His equal. And, He knew it.

"That was the beginning of a long series of events. I continue to walk on the path of destruction more determined than ever. These creatures are inferior, feeble-minded and easily manipulated. They are puppets, and I am the puppet master, pulling the strings to my liking.

"I recently learned that soon God would be sending His favorite son to this planet. I know him well. He is another loyal fool trying to please God. His mission is to save God's children and show them the way to God. If he dares to come here, I will show him no mercy. This is my kingdom and the inhabitants are my captives. I am the ruler here. It was God who placed me here and said this was my kingdom.

[26]

"From the very beginning, I vowed to destroy Earth and its inhabitants little by little...inch by inch. I will continue to generate immense hatred among God's children producing wars, killings and massive devastation. I will infiltrate God's houses of worship and cause great uproar, shame, and doubts of the existence of God. I will abolish each one of the commandments given to Moses, a so-call messenger of God. I will not cease until all that reside here on this planet curse the name of God. It is my ultimate goal."

Negativity was exceedingly moved by Lucifer's tragedy. She closed her eyes and shook her head. "I can't believe how much you have suffered," she said. She felt his immense pain, and wanted to hug him, protect him, and make things better for him. She believed that he was a victim who was wrongfully punished for wanting to do the right thing. God was responsible for Lucifer's drastic transformation and all his mishaps. He had taken everything away from him and turned him into a bitter and angry being. She was convinced that God was truly jealous of Lucifer. She admired Lucifer's audacity and strength to overcome all adversities and move on with his crusade against God. She loved him more than before and vowed to follow him to the end. His fight was now her fight; his enemies were her enemies.

From that day on, Lucifer and Negativity have been inseparable. She is faithful and supportive of Lucifer's cause. She is known to sit quietly and wait for the perfect moment to spread her destructive and poisonous seed into the minds and souls of God's beloved children. Whenever a child of God exhibits behaviors such as hopelessness, despair, anger, animosity, etc., rest assured that Negativity is close by. She is the mother of depression, self-hate, bigotry, and much more. She preys on the poor, sick, and feeble, as well as the rich and powerful. Her blind love for Lucifer has transformed her into a creature of darkness, hate, and evil. Once, flowers flourished in her presence. Now, they wither and die.

Negativity has not had any contact with her sisters since the day she left in search of Lucifer. She has severed all ties with them. She sees them as her enemies and tries to undo their good deeds. Her loyalty belongs to Lucifer, and him alone.

Lucifer and Negativity have become life partners who roam the world searching for new preys. They hide in the darkness waiting to attack their next victim. They are like hungry predators seeking victims to devour. They have pledged to continue to work together in the destruction of all humanity and love each other to the end of time.

CHAPTER 2

MARY- MOTHER OF HUMANITY

"Crucify him…death to the blasphemer and sorcerer! He must die now! He is an enemy of Caesar!" The mob frantically shouted. Jesus had been accused of claiming to be the King of the Jews.

Pontius Pilate, the Roman governor of Judaea, had finished giving the mob a choice of prisoner to be released. He was confident that the crowd would select Jesus over Barabbas, a criminal and enemy of the Rome Empire. Pontius Pilate was momentarily speechless when he heard the crowd's reaction.

"Release Barabbas! Crucify Jesus!" the mob roared repeatedly. The intensity of the mob's demands continued to escalate.

Jesus did not utter a word the entire time. He remained with his head lowered and eyes closed. It was as if he were in deep meditation.

Pontius Pilate had just finished washing his hands when he handed out the sentence. With no alternative, he said, "I sentence you to death by crucifixion." Immediately after, Pontius Pilate ordered his men to take the prisoner away and prepare for the execution.

Mary, who had been witnessing everything from afar, wept silently. It was the beginning of the final and most dreadful stage of her son's Calvary.

After being whipped, beaten, cursed, humiliated, stripped and deprived of food and water, Jesus was forced to wear a crown of thorns and carry an immense cross over his shoulder. As he moved slowly down the streets of Jerusalem, the mob shouted obscenities and mocked him.

"There goes a king without a kingdom! A want-to-be king! A ruler of nothing! Go rule over the desert creatures, your highness!" a man shouted while laughing. The people around him laughed. It was Lucifer. He and his followers were in the midst of the crowd working keenly to incite the people.

One man, feeling very brave, threw a rock. He hit Jesus hard on the shoulder, and yelled, "Death to Jesus!"

The snapping sound of a whip was heard frequently. It was coming from a Roman soldier who found immense pleasure in repeatedly flogging Jesus with full force.

"Keep moving you dirty dog!" he shouted.

Lash after lash, the whip met its target, cutting deep into Jesus' flesh, exposing the muscles and causing excessive bleeding. Although there was immense blood loss and his back was covered with severe deep lacerations, the flogging continued. No mercy was shown by any of the soldiers.

The weight of the cross and the physical exhaustion caused him to fall three times. Jesus, with swollen red eyes and gasping for air, always managed to pick himself up without uttering a word.

On one of the falls, Lucifer, disguised as an old man, approached him. He knelt and looked at Jesus. "Worship me, Jesus, and I will stop your suffering," he said.

Jesus smiled and said, "There is only one God. I will worship Him forever."

After hearing those words Lucifer vanished. Jesus continued to trudge up the hill of Golgotha. His mother, Mary, was close by.

Once again, Jesus fell to his knees. This time, Mary ran to him. Gently holding his face in her hands with infinite tenderness, she remembered the first time he fell as a young boy, and she held him in her arms to comfort him. That was so long ago. Now, she was helpless.

"My son...my son!" she whispered, as the tears streamed down her face.

Lifting his head, Jesus smiled faintly and said, "Mother, do not weep for me. I am doing God's will." Jesus rose slowly, lifted his cross, and proceeded.

A Roman soldier ordered Mary to step aside. With her hands covered with her son's blood and sweat, she stood frozen as she watched him struggle with the immensity of his burden.

Fearing that Jesus was not going to make it up the hill, a Roman soldier commanded a man from the crowd to help him carry the cross.

Mary followed not far behind her son as he climbed the hill. Her grief and desperation were weighing heavily upon her. Her torment was indescribable as she witnessed a Roman soldier pounding nails through Jesus' hands and feet and onto the wood. Blow after blow, the nails tore into the flesh of Jesus causing irreparable damage. With each pounding, Mary saw the anguish and pain on her son's face. It was more than she could bear.

The sunny sky suddenly turned dark. The sound of thunder was heard, and the rain started to come down. Spectators ran to take shelter underneath trees, while others went home.

Mary wept silently as she saw her beloved son hanging from the cross. She approached the cross and with trembling hands, she reached out to touch his feet.

A Roman soldier was about to approach her and order her to move away when another quickly stopped him. "Let her be. She is his mother. What harm can she do?" he said.

Although she was aware that the crucifixion was part of the reason why Jesus came into the world, it was not enough to stop the anguish she felt inside. If possible, she would gladly have traded places with him in order to cease his agony. However, prayer was the only option she had, so she closed her eyes and prayed.

When she opened her eyes to glance at Jesus, she noticed a serpent moving deliberately up the cross toward her son's feet. She grabbed it quickly and held it in her hand. Her immense love for her son had given her the strength to trap and immobilize it.

It was Lucifer. In his relentless pursue to destroy all dear to God, he had transformed into a serpent. Seeing Jesus nailed to the cross and vulnerable, he felt that it was the perfect opportunity to attack. The humans had destroyed the flesh. Now, it was his turn to vanquish the soul. For years, Lucifer had attempted to poison or corrupt Jesus' soul, but to no avail. Jesus' faith in God was impenetrable.

But Mary, his beloved mother, intervened. With much fortitude, Mary wiped her tears and said, "I will not allow you to harm my son's soul. You will not take his soul to imprison in your darkness. I am here to protect him. From darkness you came, and to darkness you will return." When she placed the serpent down, it moved swiftly into a hole in the ground and vanished. Lucifer was no match for the immeasurable love of a mother.

Lifting her eyes toward her son, she noticed that he had been staring at her with loving eyes. In addition to the rain, sweat and blood were pouring down his face. The final moment was approaching. Jesus addressed his mother in a voice that was barely audible, "Do not weep for me; for soon I will be with my Father in heaven. You are the mother of all humanity. Love and protect the children of God, the same way you loved and protected me. You possess the key that opens the door to new beginnings. Show them the way. Mother, thank you for all the love you have given me."

With his eyes facing the heavens, Jesus said his last words, "Father, forgive them, for they know not what they do. It is finished...into your hands I commit my spirit!" It was over.

Suddenly, there was silence. The loud chatting and laughter of the soldiers and few individuals who remained to witness the entire event ceased. Even the rain and the sound of thunder were no longer audible. Mary looked up at the dark sky. She noticed the sky opening up and two angels coming down. They had come to assist Jesus in his spiritual journey. As one of the angels carried the soul of Jesus, the other approached her. The angel smiled and uttered, "Mary, here is the key to the door of new beginnings. You are the Mother of all humanity and the way to God's kingdom. All those who believe in you will be blessed by God, the Father." He placed the key in her hand, which she tightly held. Then, he began ascending to the heavens leaving behind the lifeless body of Jesus.

As the sky closed, darkness settled in. The rain and thunder continued in full force. Staring at her son's lifeless body, Mary knew that Jesus' mission had been completed. He was on his way to be with his Father. His comforting words gave her the strength that she needed to carry on. Her mission had just begun. She would protect and love all of God's children. Moreover, she would show them the way to new beginnings. She was the mother of all humanity.

Mary's mission continued until her last day on earth. Upon her demise, those close to her noticed a key held firmly in her hand. They were perplexed about its meaning. They had never seen it before. Sensing it was of some high spiritual significance, they buried her with it.

As the body was being carried to the burial tomb, a woman from the crowd lifted her eyes towards the sky and began chanting:

[38]

"Mary, queen of all queens and mother of all mothers, pray for us in our most desperate hour of need. Blessed you are among all of God's creations. In you, He created a symbol of purity and love. Holy Mary, mother of Lord Jesus and mother of all humanity, show us the way to God's kingdom. Open the door to new beginnings so we can cleanse our bodies, minds and souls, and bathe in God's Divine light. Protect and guide us along the way as you protected and guided your son, Amen!"

Although Mary has long left the flesh, she remains very much alive helping those who seek new beginnings and the path to God's kingdom.

A mother's job never ends.

CHAPTER 3

THE FINAL BATTLE BETWEEN GOOD AND EVIL

God was staring into space as He waited for the arrival of Michael, Chief Commander of His army. He had summoned Michael to discuss a matter of great importance.

God had been observing the ongoing events on Earth for some time with much displeasure. All of His commandments had been eradicated from the conscious minds of His Earth children. Love and compassion for each other were words that no longer had meaning. For many, God had become a myth. Fewer and fewer people were attending His houses of worship. Many religious leaders preached the words of God while committing atrocities against their brothers and sisters. Crimes were being committed without any remorse or purpose. Many had sold their souls to Lucifer for the falsehood of riches and power. While others simply enjoyed living in darkness.

The magnitude of destruction and hatred had reached a high peak. God could no longer witness the devastation of all He so lovingly created. Earth was primarily designed as a learning site where His children were allowed to visit, enter a physical body, and go through a series of trials and tribulations in order to cleanse their spirits and reach a higher level of enlightenment. Instead, His children kept repeating the vicious cycle of destruction and hate.

Now the situation on Earth had reached a critical point. Lucifer had been working diligently to wreak global havoc. World leaders were preparing to go to war. The economy of powerful countries was collapsing; the lack of food, medicine and basic essential were rampant across the globe; the rich wanted more while the poor received less. Government officials, from the top to the bottom, viewed corruption as a normal act. While the compassion of politicians diminished, the suffering of the underprivileged soared.

Recently, God had gone down to Earth to speak to Lucifer. He wanted Lucifer to stop his madness and come home. He felt that Lucifer deserved another chance.

As God entered Lucifer's gloomy domain, Lucifer was there waiting for Him. God could see the venomous look in Lucifer's eyes. A once humble being, Lucifer was now a vile creature.

"My son, why do you continue to rebel against me? I have seen all you have done and where this is going.

"From the very beginning of your banishment from the kingdom, you have worked diligently to devises ways on how to hurt me. You deluded two innocent creatures into believing you were one of my messengers and eventually convincing them to eat from the forbidden tree. You turned brother against brother, and for the first time taught man how to kill. With your guidance, you instilled in men the seeds of greed, bigotry, tyranny, selfishness and destruction. You placed men as rulers of nations to do your bidding, causing mayhem around the globe. You even desecrated my houses of worship by placing your disciples to commit horrible acts on my children. Also, you have created religious extremists, corrupting their minds and convincing them to kill their brothers in my name promising them divine rewards in the afterlife. And, the list goes on. I am aware of all your malicious acts. And, now you are planning the ultimate destruction- to exterminate everyone on this planet. You have gone too far.

"Please, stop this madness. You are my son and I love you very much. Don't you realize that trying to hurt me is hurting yourself? You are a part of me," God said.

Lucifer, with much fury and poisonous rage, verbally lashed out in a defiant way. His words were full of malice and bitterness.

"I am no longer Lucifer or your son. The Lucifer you once knew does not exist. My name is Satan. You once said this was my kingdom, and so it is. I am king and master here. I bow to no one. These creatures bow to me. Your trip here has been futile. I obey no one. I am god here. I will not stop my mission until all you created is destroyed. I despise you!" Lucifer exclaimed.

"Then, you despise yourself. Remember, you are a part of me. Although you detest me, I will always love you, for you are my son," God replied.

Standing next to Lucifer was Negativity, who shyly looked away. Although she loathed God for all He did against Lucifer, she could not face Him.

"You too, Negativity?" God said while staring at her. "You were the most humble of all. Now, you have become a creature of darkness, a follower of Lucifer." Negativity remained silent, while looking away. God turned around and walked away. Before leaving He said, "I forgive you both."

As God continued to reminisce on all the occurrences involving Lucifer, His attention was suddenly diverted to the sound of footsteps moving towards the Great Hall. It was Michael.

As Michael entered the Great Hall, he noticed the look of dismay on God's celestial face. He had not seen that look since the days of Lucifer's rebellion.

"Father, you wanted to speak to me," Michael said.

"Yes, my son. The final hour has arrived," responded God.

Michael knew exactly what He was referring to. It was the moment he had been waiting and preparing for. It was the final battle between good and evil.

"Lucifer needs to be stopped as soon as possible. He has gone too far. He has created mayhem on Earth," God told Michael.

Michael bowed his head and said, "Your order is my command. I will prepare for immediate departure."

God's eyes were fixed on Michael as he walked away. The battle was about to begin.

From a distance, Michael had been following Lucifer's detrimental activities. His madness had reached an extreme and dangerous high scale. Now, it was Michael's mission to stop him.

From the beginning of time, God had been extremely loving and patient with His earthly children. Although on many occasions they had strayed from the right path and hurt Him deeply, He always forgave and showered them with immense love.

On several occasions, He had sent messengers to Earth to convey His profound disappointment and desire for them to love one another. However, things had gotten worse.

Ever since the creation of humans, Lucifer had assiduously spread the seed of hatred among God's children. Although God had given man free will to select and make choices, it was obvious that Lucifer's enticing tactics were powerful enough to convince countless numbers of individuals to walk on the dark side. He knew how to pull their strings and make them dance to his tune. He had become a master manipulator and trickster. He offered people immediate gratification while seizing their souls.

Michael began thinking of the Lucifer he once knew. They were very close and did everything together. He could not understand how or why Lucifer had turned against God. "Why is his hatred so intense toward a Father who has showered all with much love?" he thought to himself. Although he loved Lucifer still, he knew that he needed to be stopped.

It was time to get ready. Michael ordered a meeting of all soldiers. He courageously spoke to the soldiers informing them of their newly assigned mission.

"My brothers, it is my duty to inform you that we will be going to Earth to fight a battle against evil. Once again, we will be confronting Lucifer. Although he was one of the greatest soldiers in God's army, he is no longer one of us. He has vowed to annihilate all that is dear to God. Our job is to end his insanity and restore order. Prepare to leave as soon as possible."

With full combat armor, the soldiers began to get ready for their mission.

Meanwhile, Lucifer, with a beaming face and glowing eyes, was relishing the thought of his upcoming encounter with Michael. He knew Michael would be at the forefront directing God's army. Nothing gave him more pleasure than the idea of confronting Michael, his one-time brother. He would never forget that it was Michael, following God's orders, who stripped him of everything and transported him to Earth to live as an inferior being for all eternity.

Lucifer sensed that the day was rapidly approaching. From the first day that he was exiled to Earth, he had envisaged the confrontation and began preparing for the upcoming battle. He had been waiting for this battle with great anticipation.

Part of the preparation involved the gathering of lost souls and converting them into a powerful army. From the beginning of time, Lucifer had been luring humans into carrying out evil deeds. Upon their demise, the souls remained in darkness under the domination of Lucifer. He commanded them to do his will.

Lucifer was optimistic that he would defeat Michael. His army was a thousand times bigger and stronger than the previous one. He would not make the same mistake as before. He would not trust anyone. His hatred and desire for revenge made him more determined and a powerful adversary.

In addition to preparing for the upcoming battle, Lucifer was fanatically pulling the strings of world leaders and creating mayhem around the globe. A devastating war was on the verge of erupting in which weapons of mass destruction would be utilized. It was going to be a world war like no other–the extermination of humanity.

Lucifer rejoiced at his work. He had built a powerful army and created chaos among the humans. He was accomplishing all that he had set out to do.

Lucifer looked up to the sky with profound delight. He knew God was watching. "You can't stop me. I am all-powerful. You gave your love to these useless creatures and turned your back on those who truly loved you. Now, you can witness their destruction. I will destroy all that you created. Send your army. I am ready to defeat you once and for all," he shouted mockingly.

Lucifer continued savoring the moment as the final hours were approaching. His venomous laughter was causing global changes. There were reports of tidal waves, earthquakes, tsunamis, landslides, and floods occurring around the globe. Scientists and Meteorologists were baffled. They had no logical explanation. They were oblivious of the dark energy that was responsible.

Michael and his army were on their way to Earth. Upon arriving at the gates of Earth, he noticed the Earth inflamed. War among God's children had commenced. The closer he got, he could see and hear the devastating blast of massive destructive weapons. Cities were destroyed instantly. Cracks on the Earth's ocean floor were beginning to develop, causing a rise in the waters. Fires were widespread. Bodies and body parts were strewn everywhere. The scene was ghastly. As more cities and people were being extinguished, Lucifer's cynical laugh could be heard. The destruction continued without any sign of ceasing.

As Michael and his army were approaching, Lucifer could see the bright, divine aura that surrounded them. He knew it well, for he was once covered with it. He despised it and everything that came from God.

"They are here. Get ready!" Lucifer ordered his army. When Michael arrived, he was face to face with his one-time brother. He knew that the task was not going to be easy. Lucifer had gotten stronger and unyielding in his evil ways. His endless hatred for God and desire for revenge made him a powerful opponent. His only chance of defeating him was to thrust his sword into his heart.

"Once again, we meet. Give up this foolishness and enter the light. Come home. God loves you and will forgive you," Michael pleaded.

Lucifer laughed. It was a laughter filled with spitefulness. "Let me make it simple for you. I am god. I don't need anyone to forgive me. This is my Kingdom, and these are my slaves. My word is rule here. You are trespassing. I suggest you and your puppets fly back to where you came from, my one-time brother," he hollered.

Seeing that Lucifer was unrelenting, Michael pulled out his sword and swung, missing his target. Lucifer moved quickly and laughed. Undoubtedly, Lucifer had developed great speed and strength. Instantly, Lucifer retaliated. He lunged at Michael with brutal force, causing a deep gash on his arm. Lucifer's fingernails were long and sharp as a blade.

"You thought you could come here and destroy me...no, brother...I will not make the same mistake. I will never trust a brother again. This time, I will defeat you," Lucifer shouted with a malign look in his eyes.

Once more, Lucifer attacked Michael, but this time without causing injury. Michael was prepared this time. He had positioned himself in a combative stance, swinging his sword at Lucifer. One blow after another his sword met his target. Although Lucifer was struck several times, he showed no signs of being hurt. Michael had missed the heart.

Meanwhile, Michael's soldiers were engaged in combat, striking Lucifer's men with immense impact.

Michael and Lucifer continued to attack each other without any signs of defeat on either side. With one blow after another, Michael struck Lucifer's body, always missing the heart.

The opportunity Michael was waiting for finally came. Lucifer had stumbled to the ground leaving himself open and defenseless. Pinning him to the ground, Michael was about to strike the fatal blow when Lucifer managed to escape Michael's powerful grasp. Displaying signs of being injured, Lucifer, holding his right arm, fled to a nearby cave with Michael in close pursuit.

When Michael walked into the cave, he could scarcely see inside. As he continued to walk forward, a loud sound was heard. The opening of the cave had been sealed. He was standing in total darkness. He had walked into a trap.

Suddenly, he felt someone standing near him.

"Welcome, my brother. As you can see, you cannot destroy me. I am invincible."

It was Lucifer. His energy felt like that of a wild beast ready for the kill. With enormous fury, Lucifer struck a massive blow to Michael's face causing him to lose consciousness and fall to the ground.

When Michael regained consciousness and opened his eyes, he noticed that the cave was lit with torches, his sword was missing and his hands were chained. In front of him, Lucifer was sitting on his throne, surrounded by grotesque looking beings. Beside him was a woman. The woman was Lucifer's longtime companion, Negativity. She possessed the same bloodthirsty look in her eyes as Lucifer.

Lucifer signaled his slaves to bring Michael closer to him.

"How does it feel to be defenseless and alone? Where is your God now? How can you be loyal to a God who has abandoned you...a God, who shows much love to these earthly creatures and forgets those who have served and loved him? Renounce your God and show your allegiance to me, and I will be merciful. Let us be brothers once again and walk side by side," said Lucifer.

Michael, looking directly and intently into Lucifer's eyes, began to speak. "Lucifer, you are still my brother, and I love you. Please, stop this madness and come home. God is waiting for you. You were once a good and noble soldier. Release the hate from your soul and free yourself. You have lived in darkness for so long that you have forgotten what it is to walk in the light. It is true that God has given humans much love, but it

[51]

does not mean that He loves us less. Humans are like newborns. They need to be loved and nurtured. By giving them love, God is teaching them how to love one another. Because of your misguided hate, you have tried to destroy the precious gift of love by blocking God's love from entering the hearts of many. Humans cannot live without love. You can torture and imprison them, but sooner or later they will reach out to the heavens in search of God's love."

"Enough, I don't want to hear another word about your God. Because you were my one-time brother, I have been very patient with you. It ends now. Prepare to receive your punishment!" Lucifer screamed.

Michael lowered his head and closed his eyes as if praying.

"Pray all you want…Your God is not going to save you. Remember, He is too busy with His earthly children. You are dispensable, the same way I was. " Lucifer said in extreme agitation.

Abruptly, a tumultuous sound was heard followed by a violent tremor. Rocks began falling off the walls of the cave. Cracks were beginning to form on the ground–some more severe than others. Tremors upon tremors continued to cause massive damage. Each tremor was more fierce and destructive than the previous one.

Panic and desperation took over Lucifer's slaves. The cries of distress were heard all over. Some were desperately asking for God's forgiveness and intervention.

Lucifer began ruthlessly striking his victims with a whip in an attempt to regain control. "Go back you filthy worthless swine or I will personally see that you are severely chastised. I will have no clemency on you!" he exclaimed. They were like helpless beasts at the mercy of demented Lucifer.

Michael remained in his serene posture with head lowered and eyes closed during the upheaval.

Lucifer, consumed by immense rage and hate, turned to face Michael. "This is your doing...you and your God. I'll show you who is Master here." Raising his sword to strike the final blow, a blinding luminous light appeared, shielding Michael and preventing Lucifer from seeing his target. Startled and momentarily paralyzed, Lucifer's face was rigid and red with rage.

Suddenly, a figure emerged from inside the light. It was Michael. He was no longer chained. He had transformed back to his true persona. He was Michael, the angelic warrior, surrounded by a glowing aura, wearing a shining armor and holding a magnificent looking sword. Leaping forward, he plunged his sword deep into Lucifer's heart.

With a look of anguish and despair in his eyes, Lucifer dropped his sword and collapsed. Unable to regain his balance, he fell into a large opening in the ground caused by the tremors. Slowly, the streaming lava-like substance that was gushing beneath the ground began to consume

[53]

Lucifer. He desperately tried to pull himself out of the opening, however, the force of the hot lava was too overpowering.

With tears in his eyes, Michael whispered, "Farewell, my brother."

Running to the aid of her lifelong companion, Negativity shouted, "Lucifer, don't leave me!" Witnessing his demise, she closed her eyes and said, "I can't live without you." Heartbroken, she jumped into the hot lava, meeting the same fate as Lucifer.

The battle was over. Lucifer and all of his followers were defeated. It was time to go home. Michael's mission was over. As Michael ascended to the Heavens, some of his soldiers remained behind to escort Lucifer's faithful followers, who refused to repent, to a lower realm where they would linger in darkness for eternity.

None of Earth's inhabitants survived. Weapons of mass destruction eliminated the majority of the inhabitants while the remaining few died due to lack of food and water. The planet was covered with decayed bodies and body parts. The stench was nauseating. The oceans, seas, and rivers were filled with the blood of humanity. As the souls detached from their physical bodies, they roamed aimlessly in a state of confusion. Spiritual rescuers were sent to assist and direct them into the light to begin their healing process.

When all the souls were removed from the planet, a process of cleansing and purification commenced. The decayed bodies and body parts were consumed by the soil while the waters evaporated and later replaced by pure, clear liquids. The negative, dense energy that encircled the Earth's atmosphere vanished. The Earth was being primed for a new beginning. In time, Earth would be transformed into a highly elevated planet in which spiritual advanced beings would reside.

Lucifer's arrogance and rage were the cause of his downfall. Although he assumed his plan to defeat God was impregnable, he underestimated the power of God. He mistook God's love for weakness.

With the exception of a few of Lucifer's loyal followers, the majority of the souls pleaded for God's mercy and gravitated toward the light. As Michael said, "Humans (which includes the incarnate spirit) cannot live without love… sooner or later they will reach out to the heavens in search of God's love."

God is a master builder with the universe as His workspace. He will continue to create and restore. For God is God. He is everlasting.

CHAPTER 4

HE IS WATCHING US

A young man walked briskly down Main Street. He could feel the cold morning air numbing his face. The weather was brutally cold and had reached the freezing level.

He had recently moved into the neighborhood and was on his way to the Christ Baptist Church for Sunday service. It was his first time attending the church.

Upon entering the church, the frigid cold began dissipating as the warmth from the inside of the church began to settle into his body. The church was overflowing with church members. He began scanning the area for an empty seat. His eyes fell on a small space to the left side of the church. Friendly smiling faces greeted him as he moved towards the empty space.

He waited patiently for the service to commence. As he looked around, he noticed a well-groomed, distinguish looking, middle-aged man dressed in a suit and tie sitting in the front facing the crowd. Suddenly, the man got up and approached the podium. There was silence all around. He was the Pastor.

He smiled as he stood facing the crowd. He then lowered his head and focused his eyes on a bible that was situated in front of him. Placing his hands on top, he closed his eyes as if praying. After a minute or so, he opened his eyes, and then the bible. Pleased with what he saw, he sighed, looked up at the crowd and spoke. The crowd remained silent, glued to their seats eagerly waiting for the commencement of the Pastor's sermon.

"Good morning, my brothers and sisters. I would like to start by thanking the Lord for this glorious day, and to you for being here on this very cold day. God is merciful. Let us praise the Lord by saying amen."

A sea of amens filled the room. Staring at the crowd and waiting for the amens to cease, the Pastor smiled and continued. "Although it is bitter cold outside, there is immense warmth here today... thank you, Jesus."

"Amen," the crowd shouted.

"Today's sermon comes from the words of our Lord Jesus, 'Thou shall love thy neighbor as thyself, and treat others as you want to be treated.' Jesus gave us this simple yet very powerful message. By giving us this message, Jesus is teaching us how to love and respect one another. The message is about loving our brothers and sisters and treating others with respect for we are all part of God's creation."

The Pastor paused to allow the people to voice their amens.

"Amen! Thank you, Jesus," the crowd shouted. Once again, there was silence.

He continued, "Love is a gift from God that is inside all of us. We all have the capacity to love. Without love, we are empty shells roaming around in the darkness. Love helps us to come together and rise as one. It is contagious. When you love, it spreads to others and eventually comes back to you. Jesus taught us that in order to reach the kingdom of God, we must love and respect one another.

"Let take a few minutes to do an exercise. Close your eyes and imagine a beam of light representing love covering your entire being. Allow the light to grow stronger. Now, spread the light to the person sitting next to you, and eventually to the entire room."

People remained silent with their eyes closed. Soon, smiles appeared on their faces as if enjoying the experience. A few minutes later, they began jumping up and shouting, "Amen!" "Hallelujah!" and "Thank you, sweet Jesus!" In a matter a seconds, the energy in the room had skyrocketed. People began hugging and shaking each other's hands. Indeed, love had taken over.

Then, there was silence. The Pastor began to address the crowd. "Without a doubt, love is an essential element for our survival. It creates happiness and positive energy all around us. Once again, let us remember and never forget the Lord's words, 'Love thy neighbor' and treat others the way you want to be treated."

He began to read a scripture or two from the bible. At the conclusion of the reading, the Pastor stepped away from the podium and sat down. It was time for the chorus to sing. A group of talented individuals beautifully performed the songs, which contained immense praises to the Lord. After two songs, the chorus switched to a highly spirited song, which allowed the crowd to participate.

People stood up and sang out loud. The singing of the crowd created a thundering sound that filled the room. Some people began shaking uncontrollably and speaking in an incoherent language as if possessed by some unseen force. Others continued shouting, "Amen! Hallelujah! Praise the Lord!" A woman sitting next to the young man said, "The Holy Spirit has arrived." The room was electrified. When the singing stopped and the people settled in their seats, the Pastor got up and introduced a visiting Pastor.

The visiting Pastor resumed in the same manner as the Pastor, praising the Lord and reading scriptures. Both Pastors were verbally gifted and delivered uplifting sermons.

When the service was over, the young man approached the Pastor of the church and thanked him for the spiritually inspiring service.

Shaking the young man's hand, the Pastor smiled and said, "You must be new in this neighborhood. I have never seen you before."

"Yes, I recently moved here," replied the young man.

"Welcome to the house of God. Come again, my son," the Pastor responded.

The young man said his farewells, and walked away. As he strolled down the street, he smiled feeling contented with the morning's event.

He had recently moved into the neighborhood because of its diverse religious organizations. He found the area to be unique and stimulating. A Spiritualist Church was just a couple of blocks away from the Christ Baptist Church. A short distance from the Spiritualist Church was a Roman Catholic Church. A Mosque, a Buddhist Temple, a Hindu Temple, and a Synagogue were spread out but accessible. His mission was to visit each one. He was like an archeologist ready to explore new finds.

A few months had passed by when the young man ran into the Pastor from the Christ Baptist church.

"Hello. Where have you been, my son? I have not seen you in Sunday services. You attended once and never returned. Have you forgotten Our Lord Jesus?" the Pastor asked.

The young man smiled kindly and said, "No, I have not. I have been visiting all of God's houses of worship in the neighborhood. It has been a fascinating and valuable experience."

The Pastor, disguising his displeasure, replied, "Son, why search for God elsewhere, when you can find Him in our church. You are wasting valuable time and energy by visiting these other places. The true path to the kingdom of God is through our church. In our church, you will find true salvation. Be aware that Satan likes to play tricks on people in order to keep them away from the righteous path to God. I feel he is pulling you away from God's divine light."

The young man listened attentively without uttering a word. The Pastor continued to speak.

"The other day, I saw you entering the Spiritualist Church on Henry

Street. The Bible warns us that we should not attempt to contact spirits for there are great spiritual dangers in doing so. God clearly tells us that it is impossible for us to contact spirits. It is another one of Satan's ploys to deviate man from reaching the kingdom of God. If you continue to visit the Spiritualist church, you will definitely be in his clutches."

The Pastor paused, as if waiting for the young man to respond. Instead, the young man remained silent.

The Pastor resumed, "Next Sunday we are having a special service. We will be baptizing new members. I would like for you to join us. Have you ever been baptized, my son?"

"Yes, a long time ago," replied the young man.

"What was the name of the church?" asked the Pastor.

"It was not a church. Several people gathered at a river where a humble man baptized us in the name of God," he responded.

"What was the man's title?" the Pastor inquired.

"The man did not possess any titles," the young man answered.

The Pastor was appalled. His eyes widened as he stared at the young man. "You were not baptized, my son. The man was a charlatan and an instrument of Satan. I am afraid you were deceived."

The young man remained calm as he responded, "With all due respect, I disagree. The man was neither a charlatan nor an instrument of

Satan. He was a man of God doing God's work."

By now, the Pastor was no longer able to disguise his annoyance. "Nonsense, the man was a charlatan. He was not affiliated to any church and had no credentials. How can you believe in such a man?" the Pastor asked in a sharp tone.

Once again, the young man waited patiently for the Pastor to finish his statement. Then, he calmly replied, "I believed in the man because he was a pure soul, devoted to spreading the word of God to all. God does not measure men by their credentials or the church they belong to. He looks into their hearts and determines their worth. God knows…"

The Pastor rudely interrupted him and said, "I have been a Pastor for twenty five years. I know what I am talking about. You have been misled."

The Pastor reached into his coat pocket and retrieved a small size bible. He began reciting a passage.

"Watch out for false prophets. They come to you in sheep's clothing, but inwardly they are ferocious wolves. By their fruit, you will recognize them. Do people pick grapes from thorn bushes, or figs from thistles? Likewise, every good tree bears good fruit, but a bad tree bears bad fruit. A good tree cannot bear bad fruit, and a bad tree cannot bear good fruit. Every tree that does not bear good fruit is cut down and thrown into the fire. Thus, by their fruit you will recognize them. Matthew 7:15-23."

The young man politely waited for the Pastor to stop speaking.

Steadily gazing at the Pastor, the young man calmly said, "Are you saying that a man who lacks credentials or membership of a bona fide church is not worthy of being an instrument of God? That such a person is an instrument of Satan and/ or a false prophet. Was your sermon of, 'Treat others the way you want to be treated, or Love thy neighbor as thyself' done in vain? It seems you give more importance to the person's outer presentation and not to the person's inner feelings and true love for God. How or where you worship God is not important. What is important is to worship God. He does not care if you worship Him in a lavish church or an impoverished broken down building. You can worship him anywhere for He is everywhere. He sees and hears all. God did not speak to Moses in one of the lavish temples of Egypt. He chose to speak to him in an isolated area in Mount Horeb. Why is it that God selects his messengers from the most humble of men and not those who are well versed or possess credentials? Whether you are Baptist, Catholic, Jewish, Muslim, Buddhist, Hindu, or Spiritist, you all belong to God's family. You are all his children, and He loves you all the same.

"As for contacting spirits, you said, 'the bible warns us that we should not attempt to contact spirits for there are great spiritual dangers in doing so.' If you believe that to be true, then why do you call upon Jesus and God, the Father? Aren't they spirits? Haven't you ever sat down and mentally spoken to a departed loved one as if they were near and said to them how you missed them and wished that they were here?

Is that not spirit communication? What harm is that? What do you have to say about the Catholics who pray to the spirits of the saints, the Hindus who pray to the Goddesses, etc.? Are they all part of Satan's conspiracy? If you believe that God gave the Ten Commandments to Moses, then you would know what is important to God and what is not. At no point did He say, 'Thou shall not communicate with spirits.' God has many spirit messengers. They are called guardian angels and spirit guides. Some people refer to them as spirits of light.

"A poor, illiterate, humble man with a pure heart is more likely to enter the kingdom of God than a scholar with much insight on biblical passages."

The Pastor's nostrils were flaring and heart was pounding. The young man's discourse irritated him. He looked at him with vexation and rage. "Who are you and what right do you have to preach to me on matters of God or the bible? I have been a Pastor for twenty five years and possess degrees in religious studies," he exclaimed.

The young man respectfully interrupted the Pastor. "It is true that I am not a Pastor or possess any secular titles. I possess nothing, and yet I possess all. My greatest possession is my love for God. You asked me who I am and what right do I have to speak to you about God? I am simply a humble man who has been called by many names. Some call me the shepherd, a prophet, a holy man, and the messiah. And many know me as the Son of God."

"You are insane!" the Pastor yelled.

The young man looked at him tenderly and said, "I am Jesus."

Suddenly, the Pastor's heart began beating faster and sweat began pouring down his face. His knees started shaking. He lost his balance and fell to the ground. Jesus reached out to help him. As the Pastor grabbed his hand, he saw the mark on Jesus' hand where the nail had penetrated.

The Pastor became speechless and motionless as he stood in front of Jesus. He was stunned. Although he had always been a man of many words, he could not find one word to express adequately what he was feeling. He was having a difficult time comprehending what was happening. His mind was a complete blank.

"I am the one who you call out to and praise every Sunday. I am Jesus who was baptized by John. It is true that John the Baptist was not a member of any temple. His temple was in his heart. He possessed no material wealth; however, he was rich in spiritual blessings. Although he possessed no credential, his knowledge and approval came from above. He was a simple, humble man who loved God with all his heart and was blessed by God. He was a true messenger of God."

Unexpectedly, the young man transformed into the divine image of Jesus. A luminous light covered his face, while his eyes were magnetic and penetrating. The Pastor gazed at him with profound awe. He could not believe what was happening in front of him. Once again, he was on the ground. This time, he was on his knees sobbing. It was as if he was asking for forgiveness. He was in the presence of divine greatness.

Jesus smiled and in a tone of immense tenderness said, "I am Jesus. Do not forget my teachings. Remember to respect and love others no matter how they choose to worship God. For you are all His children. I will be watching." Then Jesus began fading away slowly.

The Pastor, moved by all that had occurred, wept profusely. He had been tested and failed shamefully. His ego and unyielding ways blinded him. He had challenged Jesus unknowingly. As he got up and walked away, he kept hearing the words of Jesus, "I will be watching."

The Pastor, bathed in tears, walked into his church. It was empty and quiet. He walked to the front of the church and sat down.

"Oh, my Lord, I have failed you. Please, forgive me. I was a blinded fool. I vow to embrace all of God's children no matter what religion they observe," he said, as tears continued to pour down his face.

From that moment, he no longer viewed each religion as being separate or inferior. Instead, he saw them as one unit linked together under God.

During Sunday services, the Pastor's sermons were full of compassion, love and respect for all. The words poured out of him with much ease. He was not just saying them; he was practicing what he was preaching. He embraced all of his brothers and sisters with love and respect no matter what religious background they were from, and directed the members of his church to do the same.

Every Sunday, he concluded the service saying, "Remember, Jesus is watching us."

cfcordova 1/15

CHAPTER 5

SPIRIT ATTACHMENT

"Mommy, help me!" the little girl screamed. Her name was Lucy, and she just woke up from a horrific dream. She was five years old. This was her first encounter with a malevolent energy that would plague her in the coming years.

Lucy's parents rushed to her side upon hearing her cries. Lucy was trembling with a look of fear in her eyes. She was soaked in sweat from head to toe. While the father stayed near the door, the mother sat beside Lucy comforting her.

"A bad man was chasing me. He was a monster and had blood on his face. He said he was going to hurt me." Lucy told her mother as tears ran down her face.

Lucy's mother, Elizabeth, grabbed her and placed Lucy's head on her chest. "Everything is going to be okay. Mommy and daddy are here. No one is going to hurt you," Elizabeth assured her.

The following morning, Lucy remembered nothing of the nightmare. It was as if it had never occurred. Her parents never mentioned or questioned Lucy about the incident. It was completely forgotten.

Lucy was the only child of Elizabeth and Sam. After several miscarriages, Elizabeth and Sam were blessed with a beautiful baby girl. She had her mother's black curly hair and her father's big brown eyes. They adored her. She was their princess.

From a very young age, Lucy demonstrated an extraordinary talent for dancing. She attended ballet school and excelled. Although she loved doing other activities children her age were involved in, her true passion was dancing.

Lucy attended her first spiritual gathering when she was ten years old. Lucy's aunt, Josephine, the oldest of the sisters, invited Elizabeth to attend a spiritual session with her. At first, she refused. She was a non-believer of spirit communication and felt it was a waste of time. However, her sister was adamant and would not take no for an answer. Elizabeth finally agreed to accompany her sister. Two days later, Josephine, Elizabeth, and Lucy were on their way to the gathering.

It was one o'clock in the afternoon when they arrival. Josephine knocked on the door and waited. A tall heavy set, jovial woman opened the door. Her name was Luz. She hugged and kissed Josephine as if delighted to see her.

"Come in. It is nice to see you again. Where have you been?" Luz said.

"I was out of town on business. I'll tell you more later on. This is my sister, Elizabeth and her daughter, Lucy," Josephine replied.

"Glad to meet you. You have a pretty little girl. Make yourself at home," Luz said.

Luz directed them into the back room where the session would take place. When they walked in, they were greeted by several people who were sitting around the room. In the middle of the room were a table with a white tablecloth and chairs around it. On top of the table was a medium size clear fish bowl filled with water. There was also a cross, two books, candles and a bottle with a mixture of water, fragrance and herbs. In the corner of the room, on top of a chest, the aroma of frankincense was coming from a pot of burning incense. The room had a peaceful and relaxing ambience.

They sat down and waited for the session to commence. A few more people entered the room. Some, dressed in white, sat at the table while others sat in empty seats around the room. When Luz walked in, she sat at the head of the table. With a pleasant and inviting smile, Luz asked Josephine to sit at the table. Josephine, who was a medium in the initial stage of mediumship development, gladly accepted and sat next to Luz.

After lighting a candle, Luz grabbed one of the books, closed her eyes and said the Our Father prayer. The book was called *The Gospel According to Spiritism* by Allan Kardec. When she opened the book, she smiled as if pleased with what she saw.

"Today's reading comes from Chapter 12: Love Your Enemies-Discarnate Enemies," she said.

"…As children correct themselves of their defects, so the evil man or woman will one day recognize their errors and so gradually become good people. The Spiritist also knows that death is only a relief from the material presence of the enemy because this enemy can continue to pursue with hate even after leaving the Earth. Our enemies in the invisible world manifest themselves and their malice by means of obsession and subjugations, as can frequently be seen…" she read.

Luz finished reading the chapter and placed the open book on the side of the table. She looked around and said, "We must love our enemies whether they are in the flesh or out of it. Jesus taught us to forgive and love our enemies. Hate can only create more hate, even in the after-life."

Everyone was attentive listening to Luz except Elizabeth. She had closed her eyes as if bored.

Luz grabbed another book. It was a book of prayers. After reading a few prayers, Luz instructed the mediums to hold hands and close their eyes.

"Dear Father, allow your spirit messengers to embrace us with your Divine light and wisdom. If we are unworthy of your Divine light, forgive us and show us the way to you. If there is anyone here with impure thoughts, allow your spirit messengers to penetrate their hearts and minds, and assist them to see your Divine greatness. May the mediums push away their egos and maintain a pure aura. In your hand, we place our bodies and souls. May your will be done," Luz exhorted.

The mediums were ready to commence the spiritual work. They began sprinkling some of the prepared liquid mixture on their heads and bodies. Each one, in an orderly manner, got up and repeated the procedure. Some began shaking as they cleansed themselves. When all the mediums were seated, there was absolute silence. The mediums sat with their eyes closed waiting for the entities to arrive. Moments later, some of the mediums began bonding with their spirit guides. The work had begun.

One of the mediums kept fidgeting around her chair as if something was bothering her. Suddenly, she looked up and pointed at Elizabeth. A woman sitting next to Elizabeth tapped her on her shoulder and whispered, "The woman is referring to you."

Elizabeth looked up and waited for the woman to speak. Meanwhile, Lucy had fallen asleep.

"You are the mother of the child sitting next to you, am I correct?"

"Yes, she's my daughter," Elizabeth replied while avoiding eye contact.

"Please, stand," the medium said.

Elizabeth slowly got up. She was not pleased that she was requested to stand up. Her body remained tense and rigid throughout the verbal encounter. In the interim, Lucy woke up thinking it was time to leave.

The medium looked directly at Lucy and then Elizabeth. After a minute or so, the medium began to speak. "There is a dark, negative energy attached to your daughter. It is an energy from a past life. The spirit claims that your daughter belongs to him. He is obsessed by the idea of revenge. Also, he is saying that he is going to make her pay the debt that is owed to him."

Not understanding a word of what the medium was saying,

Elizabeth began to feel agitated. She kept avoiding eye contact with the medium.

The medium continued after a brief pause. "Although you are not a believer of spirits or reincarnation, it is important for you to know that your daughter needs proper spiritual help in order to detach the energy from her. Today, we will begin with prayers, but it is crucial that you and your daughter continue to attend these sessions. We need to appeal to God for His help in order to work with this energy."

The group began to pray asking for God's divine intervention. As the group continued to pray, the medium asked Elizabeth's permission to allow Lucy to come forward. Josephine looked at her sister and said, "It's okay." Lucy got up, went to the front table and stood next to her aunt. The medium began giving Lucy spiritual passes in an attempt to free her from some of the negative energy.

"I am transmitting spiritual energy that comes from God's spirit messengers to detach some of the negative energy that surrounds your daughter," she told Elizabeth. At first, Lucy seemed frightened. However, the medium's tender touch, warm smile and comforting words helped Lucy to relax.

"Don't worry, my child, everything is going to be fine," the medium told Lucy.

Elizabeth insisted in leaving immediately when the session ended. Outside she expressed her displeasure to her sister. "Spirit attachment is just ridiculous. How can you believe in such nonsense?" she questioned her sister. She vowed never to return. Even though Josephine attempted to explain, Elizabeth refused to listen.

A few years had passed from the day of the gathering. Elizabeth had kept her vow and never returned. Meanwhile, Lucy had blossomed into a beautiful young girl, who continued to excel in her academic studies, as well as dancing.

When she was fifteen years old, she had a terrifying dream. In the dream, a sinister looking man kept her shackled and imprisoned. As he violently dragged her along desolated fields, he kept saying, "You belong to me." When she woke up, she was trembling and sweating profusely. Her heartbeat was racing. The dream was so vivid.

Distressed, Lucy approached her mother, who was in the kitchen preparing breakfast. "Mom, I had a horrible dream last night. I feel as if I have seen the man before. However, I can't remember," Lucy told her mother.

"It was just a nightmare. People have them. It's nothing for you to worry about. It doesn't mean anything. Have some breakfast and you'll feel better," her mother said nonchalantly. There was no further mention of the dream.

Lucy's life was going fantastically. She had graduated from high school and was attending college. She also continued to excel in her dancing skills. The details of her past dream were a faded memory.

College generated many happy moments for Lucy. One of those moments was when she met Phil. He was a handsome young man who was a college senior. According to Lucy, it was love at first sight. They immediately fell in love. Soon, they were talking about marriage. When she revealed their intentions, her parents were somewhat displeased. They wanted her to finish college first. She continued to insist until her parents finally gave in. They were married a few months after Phil graduated from college. She appeared to be the happiest girl in the world.

On her wedding night, Lucy saw two eyes staring at her in the dark. Frightened by the apparition, she immediately reached out to Phil. When she told him what she had seen, his behavior was comparable to her mother. He smiled and assured her that it was the reflection of the light from outside.

That night, she had a dream similar to the one she had years before. She saw herself shackled and crying for mercy. She could sense the man's imperishable hate. With much venom in his words, he uttered, "You will never find happiness...I promise you that." She woke up terrified. Phil was sound asleep. She sat on the edge of the bed wondering what it all meant. After a short while, she felt asleep.

Lucy began to feel restless after two months of marriage. The happiness she once felt had disappeared. She felt that her life was empty and unfulfilling. However, she continued to play the role of a good wife.

Phil, who worked full time and attended grad school at night, was a dedicated husband. Although she was not interested in going back to school, Phil encouraged her to take dancing classes and pursue a dancing career. He wanted to see her happy.

Six months later, she became pregnant. She thought the baby would be the solution to her problem. But, she was wrong.

Lucy gave birth to a beautiful baby girl. Everyone, except for Lucy, was overjoyed. Although she loved her daughter, it was not enough to fill the emptiness she felt deep inside.

She resumed playing the role of the happy wife and mother the first few months. Nevertheless, her feelings of discontent continued to intensify. Not being able to prolong the pretense, she decided to leave.

While her husband and baby slept, Lucy kissed her daughter, gathered her belongings, grabbed money she had saved, placed a note on the kitchen table, and walked away. Not once did she look back or wonder if she was doing the right thing. She just kept walking into the darkness of the night.

A friend took her in. She began working an evening job and

attending auditions in the daytime. She was determined to become a dancer. When she saved enough money, she acquired her own apartment. Although she was free to pursue her goals, a sense of inner sadness was always present.

Lucy finally got her first break after many months of attending auditions. A traveling dance company hired her to be one of their dancers. She was in her glory. Life was smiling on Lucy. She was getting the opportunity to achieve two of her goals–to dance with a prestigious dance company and travel around the world.

Occasionally, she would call her mother for a brief update. However, when her mother began sermonizing, she would hang up quickly. She was living her life and did not want anyone to interfere. Her husband, as well as her father, refused to have any contact with her. Her father, who loved her dearly, was disgusted by her behavior. He could not comprehend why she would leave a wonderful husband and newborn baby.

After two years of traveling across the globe with the dance company, Lucy's life changed once more. The lead dancer had an accident that left her immobile, and Lucy was selected to replace her. The opportunity she waited for had arrived.

Her first solo performance was superb. Everyone wanted to know who she was. She had gone from being anonymous to identifiable. She had attained her aspiration.

Every performance was done with the highest perfection. She

continued to receive many accolades wherever she went. Although she was on top of her profession, she still felt incomplete and empty.

She went from one relationship to another searching for happiness, but to no avail. Each relationship was short-lived. Everyone adored Lucy, the dancer, but no one took the time to know Lucy, the person.

The more she searched for happiness and companionship, the more lonely and unloved she felt. On several occasions, she would look at herself in the mirror, with tears in her eyes, and ask herself, "Why can't I be happy?"

Her dreams were becoming more frequent and disturbing. The scenario was always the same–chained, dragged, and an ominous laughter. "What does it all mean?" she wondered.

She began visiting a psychotherapist in an attempt to get answers and mental comfort. After numerous sessions, she witnessed no change. Her dreams were consistent, and her depression was intensifying. The therapist, convinced that her problems stemmed from unresolved family issues, suggested she revisit her family and confront her past. Additionally, the therapist felt that her dreams and depression were the results of inner feelings of guilt connected to her abandonment of her family.

Lucy had not revisited her past since the day she walked away. Not even for the death of her parents did she return. Although she loved them, she could not bear facing the errors of her past behaviors. She believed that by staying away, she was protecting herself from unwanted encounters.

Now, Lucy was considering the notion of returning home to face her demons. She needed to put an end to her depression and nightmares. Because of a recent knee injury and bouts of depression, she had taken a sabbatical from dancing.

Lucy had returned home, and no one was around to greet her. Her husband had remarried, and her daughter was in high school. She tried communicating with her daughter on several occasions, but was rejected. Her daughter refused to establish any kind of relationship with her.

Josephine, Lucy's aunt, was praying in front of a small homemade altar. With her eyes closed and focused on her prayers, she heard a voice whispering in one of her ears. "She is coming home. You must help her." Bewildered by what was said to her, Josephine questioned the entity. No answer was given.

The following day, the phone rang. "Hello, Aunt Josephine. It's me, Lucy," the voice on the phone said. Upon hearing the voice, Josephine was in a state of stupor. Several years had passed since the last time she spoke to Lucy. In fact, she remembered it well. It was when Elizabeth had passed away. Lucy had called to say she could not make it. Josephine was furious and gave her a piece of her mind.

Josephine listened with much caution to Lucy. During the conversation, Josephine recalled the words that were said to her the day before, "She is coming. You must help her." The spirit was referring to Lucy.

Even though Josephine disagreed with Lucy's behavior, she never stopped loving her. "Come tomorrow. I'll wait for you here. See you tomorrow," Josephine said as she ended the conversation.

The next day, the doorbell rang. It was Lucy. When Josephine opened the door, she saw much sadness in Lucy's eyes. In addition, she noticed that Lucy had lost a lot of weight. They embraced and held each other for a long time. Both had tears in their eyes. Lucy walked in and sat down.

"How are you?" Josephine asked.

"I could be better," Lucy replied.

After sharing the details of her career and travels, Lucy told Josephine the real reason why she was back. "I came back to face my demons," Lucy said.

Josephine, who had been listening attentively, suggested that perhaps her demons were of a spiritual involvement. Although Lucy was never a spiritual person, the suggestion gave her something to consider. Furthermore, Josephine offered to take her to a spiritual gathering the following week.

After several hours of reminiscing, Lucy got up, hugged her aunt and said, "See you next week." She walked away feeling a bit alleviated.

She had released some of her darkest fears concerning her dreams.

Lucy called her aunt the following week. "Hi. I am just calling to let you know that I won't be going to the gathering today. I have a severe headache. I just want to stay in and relax. Perhaps, next time."

Josephine responded adamantly, "You are being manipulated by the energy. I want you to take two aspirins and get ready. I'll be there in fifteen minutes."

Knowing that her aunt could be very persistent, she got up, took two aspirins and got dressed.

When Josephine arrived at Lucy's hotel room, she began explaining the spiritual process to Lucy. "It is important to have faith and maintain a positive outlook."

Lucy was a bit anxious as she and her aunt traveled to the gathering. It was many years since her first visit to a spiritual gathering. When they arrived, Lucy noticed that the place was not the same one she had visited as a child. "This is not the same place we visited when I was young," she stated.

"No, it's not. Luz passed away a few years ago. This is Marie's place. She used to attend the gatherings in Luz's apartment. I don't know if you remember her," Josephine replied.

As they approached the apartment, an inviting aroma of myrrh and frankincense roamed the hallway. Josephine knocked on the door and waited. She heard a voice on the other side saying, "Coming...Give me one minute."

Suddenly, a young girl opened the door. She was approximately seventeen with long black hair and a welcoming smile.

"Come in," she said warmly.

Josephine and Lucy walked in and stood by the door waiting for Marie to appear. Marie quickly appeared and greeted them. "Hi, I am running a bit late but make yourselves at home," she uttered.

The young girl was Marie's daughter, Sonia. Following her Mother's orders, she took Josephine and Lucy to the living room. Several people were already seated. They were very cordial when Lucy and Josephine entered the room.

The same setting that was in Luz's home was displayed: a table, chairs, books, candles, a cross, a liquid bottle with herbs inside and a clear bowl filled with water were in order.

Some of the mediums were sitting at the table. Shortly, the other mediums arrived and took their seats. Marie and her daughter were the last ones to be seated. After saying a short opening prayer, Marie took one of the books and told Lucy to close her eyes, pray, and open the book. Lucy's heartbeat raced as she took the book. She felt a high level of apprehension. She had performed in front of hundreds of people and never once did she experience such uneasiness.

After opening the book, she gave it back to Marie. Her hands were shaking and moist.

Lucy had opened the book to chapter 12, Love Your Enemies from *The Gospel According to Spiritism* from Allan Kardec. The same chapter that was read many years ago in Luz's home.

After reading the chapter, and giving a brief explanation, Marie commenced reading several prayers from a prayer book. By now, the atmosphere in the room was extremely comforting. Lucy, who was nervous at first, was feeling a sensation of calmness. During the prayers, she closed her eyes and asked God for guidance. Unexpectedly, her eyes got teary and she wanted to cry for some unapparent reason. She sat quietly and continued to pray.

The mediums had begun to prepare their bodies. Some were connecting with their spirit guides while others prayed silently.

Sonia was now under the influence of her spirit guide. The entity began speaking through her. "Good day. May God's blessings and peace be with all of you here. I have come to cleanse the medium for there will be much spiritual work here today. It is important for all of you to maintain focus and be in constant prayer. May God's light continue to shine on all of us. Peace be here," the entity said.

When the spirit left, Sonia remained in a daze. She looked around and fixed her gaze on Lucy. A few minutes later, an unfamiliar force had taken over Sonia's body. Her facial expression and tone of voice had changed. The young girl was possessed by a dark energy that was highly enraged. "Why are you here? Do you think that by being here, these people are going to save you?" the energy said to Lucy in a taunting tone.

Marie directed Lucy to stand, but not to speak to the entity. As Lucy got up, she could feel her legs wobbling and her heart throbbing. Lucy could not comprehend why the energy that was coming through was familiar to her. She felt she knew the energy well. "But, how could that be?" she asked herself.

Momentarily, the energy disengaged from Sonia's body. As Sonia was recovering from the spiritual encounter, Marie began speaking to Lucy. "There is a negative energy around you. It is the energy of a spirit from a past life. He is seeking revenge and has attached himself to you. He says he will not leave until all debts are paid in full." She then directed the group to pray silently.

Once again, the energy had taken possession of Sonia's body. With a tone full of hostility, the words came out of the medium's mouth. "You will never be happy. I will make you pay for everything you did. Don't pretend you don't remember me? You can conceal your evilness from others, but l know who you really are. I was one of your slaves. The one you found immense pleasure in torturing. Because of your sadistic and demonic acts, I decided to escape. I was unsuccessful in doing so. I was captured, chained, and dragged back to the plantation. There, I was restrained to a tree and whipped savagely. As a punishment to me, and a warning to all your slaves, you had my wife and five-year-old daughter burned alive."

There was a brief pause. A tear rolled down Sonia's face. Then, with a tone of immense resentment, the energy resumed. "As the whip continued to cut deep into my skin, I was forced to hear their cries for mercy, witness their bodies being consumed by the fire and smell their scorched flesh. I called out to God and made a vow to seek revenge. You laughed and ordered your men to skin me alive and feed my flesh to your dogs. Inch by inch, they cut and pulled off my skin while you stood nearby and watched without remorse. Slowly, I began losing strength and could no longer scream out for mercy. I took my last breath and came out of the body. My spirit remained in the area witnessing the devastation of my flesh. At the end, only pieces of flesh hanging from a lifeless skeleton were the only thing that remained. Spirits of light were calling me to enter the light, but I refused. I roamed in darkness waiting for the opportunity to seek my revenge. I have followed you from lifetime to lifetime causing you extreme unhappiness. And, I will continue to do so for all eternity. You are chained to me and will never escape. I will not rest until the debt is paid in full. I will never release you. Do you hear me? Never...never...never!"

The medium opened her eyes slowly. She looked around as if unfamiliar with her surroundings. After a minute or two, her spirit guide came through and proceeded to give her spiritual passes.

Meanwhile, Lucy, who had been emotionally moved by his story, was weeping silently. Although part of her felt she was not capable of such atrocities, another part of her felt the weight of her guilt.

Lucy was taken to the front table where she was directed to sit. One of the mediums began giving her passes. As the medium continued to work on her, Lucy found herself drifting away.

At first, she saw a woman laughing and a man begging for mercy. Then, she was transported to a gloomy place. There, she heard the sound of thunderous laughter coming from nowhere. The sound continued to get louder and louder. Suddenly, a heinous looking face appeared. A fragment of the face was bloody and ripped apart while other parts revealed facial bones. Its eyes were fixed on her. There was no one around to help her. She was trapped. Her desperation was increasing by the second.

"Lucy...Lucy. Come back!" It was the voice of the medium who was tenderly holding Lucy's hands. She was calling Lucy to return. As she opened her eyes tears began pouring down her face. She had traveled to a dark and unknown place.

Too weak to move, Lucy remained seated. The mediums, as well as the people in attendance, began praying. As the prayers continued, Lucy felt a pulling sensation. It was as if some unpleasant energy was being pulled out of her. She closed her eyes and prayed.

By the end of the evening, Lucy was feeling better. Marie gave her the name of a prayer book for her to purchase. She jotted down the name of the prayers she needed to do every night. The list consisted of The Spirit Guides prayer, Forgiveness prayer, An Obsessed Spirit prayer, and Unrepentant Souls prayer. When the gathering ended, Lucy thanked everyone and promised to return.

Lucy stayed overnight at her aunt's place. They chatted for hours. She was entranced by all the details of the gathering. There was so much information she wanted to know.

"I have never experienced anything like that before," Lucy told her aunt.

Josephine looked at her lovingly and said, "It's going to be alright. Just have faith in God, and He will help you find your way out of the darkness."

For the first time, in a long time, Lucy slept like a baby. The next morning, she felt emotionally uplifted.

The entire week, Lucy did her prayers faithfully. Each time, she experienced the same inner calmness and joy. That week, she had two similar dreams. She saw herself standing in the middle of a poorly lit room. There were two men standing next to her. One of the men was familiar to her. He was the man who had chained and dragged her across the fields. The other man was dressed in white surrounded by a luminous light. He looked similar to the pictures she had seen in church of Jesus. She noticed that in each dream, she was neither shackled nor dragged. Moreover, the loud sound of the ominous laughter was no longer heard. Upon awakening, she experienced an overall sensation of calmness.

Lucy waited with much anticipation for the day of the next spiritual gathering. When the day of the gathering arrived, Lucy was overjoyed. She could not wait to share the events of the week with the mediums.

Lucy and her aunt arrived at the spiritual gathering a bit early. They were warmly welcomed by the mediums who were already there.

As Lucy began to share her week-long experience, Marie smiled and said, "God is so merciful. Follow the path that is in front of you, and you will experience true happiness."

The spiritual gathering started in its normal fashion. After the completion of prayers and the passing of spirit guides, one of the mediums began to incorporate the spirit connected to Lucy. He appeared less bitter and more rational.

"I am beginning to understand many things. The spirits who surround me are showing me the errors of my ways. I am not fully convinced. I don't want to speak any more...good bye."

The gathering continued without any more manifestation of the spirit.

Lucy and her aunt attended faithfully the gatherings for many weeks without any word or sign from the spirit. With each visit, she was feeling happier and whole. She no longer felt the inner void that had weighed her down for many years.

One day, while attending the gathering, a voice of humility was heard coming out of the mouth of one of the mediums. It was the spirit connected to Lucy.

"Greetings. I come asking for forgiveness. My spirit has come face to face with the ugliness it possesses. I was so consumed with my thirst for revenge that I saw nothing else. I lived in darkness. I am told that God will forgive me for I am one of his children who seeks His divine light. With the help of these spirit friends, I am in the process of healing. There is still much work ahead of me. However, I feel comfort in knowing that I am on the right path to God. I have learned to release my anger and bitterness by replacing it with love. I feel free. I ask for your forgiveness. I need to detach and release myself from these chains. They are the same chains I had placed on you. It is time for me to depart and move on. My mission will take time, but it is better to start now than never. I hope you will remain on the path to God. I leave in these waters all the pain and suffering I had placed in your path. I also place here these chains. I release you and set you free. May God forgive me for all my transgressions and take me into his arms. Goodbye."

When the spirit left, there was a feeling of sadness in the air. Everyone began to prayer silently.

"I forgive you, and I hope you and God can forgive me for all the pain I had caused you," Lucy said. She wept as never before.

In an attempt to comfort her, one of the mediums held her hand and said, "Cry all you want for the tears are cleansing your soul. You are unlocking the invisible chains that kept you a prisoner in darkness for so long."

By the end of the gathering, Lucy felt as if she had emerged from the very depths of hell. She felt a sensation of peacefulness that she had never experienced before.

Moved by all that had transpired, Lucy revealed to Josephine, "For the first time, I feel free."

Lucy's dance career had ceased after knee surgery. She was no longer able to move with such poise during her dance routines. Instead of being dejected, she accepted her fate with much love and resignation. In fact, she savored the idea of beginning a new life.

With the money she had saved, she purchased an apartment and opened a small dance studio for young girls. She even convinced her aunt to move in with her. For the first time in her life, she was experiencing true happiness.

Lucy continued to attend the gatherings at Marie's place. In time, she developed her mediumship and was one of the mediums of the gatherings.

During the gatherings, she learned that her daughter was the incarnate spirit of the five-year-old girl she had ordered to be burned alive. With much love and patience, Lucy was finally able to reunite with her daughter. Now, married and with a child, her daughter was able to forgive her mother. Lucy knew that the forgiveness was not only for abandoning her in this lifetime, but for past life offenses.

At the age of sixty, Lucy passed away from heart failure. When her spirit stepped out of the body, her tormentor was not waiting for her as he did many times in the past. Instead, there were spirits of light waiting to guide her into the light. Indeed, she was free.

CHAPTER 6

THE MESSENGER

Aditya arrived home after a long day of working in the fields. The sun was slowly fading away, and darkness was settling in. The children were playing outside and Maya, eight months pregnant, was resting in bed.

He lovingly greeted his children and walked into his home. It was a one-room shack that had no electricity or running water. Candles and two lanterns lit the room. When he approached Maya, he noticed that she was sweating profusely and moaning. When she turned her head to look at him, he noticed a look of desperation on her face.

"Thank God you are here. The baby wants to come out early. Go and fetch the midwife. Please, hurry," she murmured.

Without uttering a word, he placed his tools down and ran out the door. The midwife lived just a few houses away.

It was Maya's third pregnancy. However, this pregnancy was completely different from the other two. With the first two pregnancies, she experienced severe nausea, fatigue, dizziness, swollen ankles, and mood swings. This time, she felt none of the above. Instead, she felt a sense of euphoria and immense energy. On many occasions, Aditya had to tell her to slow down and remind her that she was pregnant.

Now, things were proceeding quickly. The unborn child was in a rush to come into the world and refused to wait the full term.

"Oh, Divine Mother Durga, help me!" Maya prayed, as the sweat poured down her face. The time had come, and she could not wait for the midwife.

The children entered and went to her side. Although they were young, six and seven years old, they tried to console her by holding and caressing her forehead and hands. Grabbing tightly to the bed cover, Maya began to push. Maya took a deep breath and pushed hard. In a matter of seconds, the baby had come out. It was a girl.

Aditya had just arrived with the midwife when he saw Maya holding the baby. The midwife rushed to her side to assist. However, what she saw left her in awe. There was a white glowing light encircling the baby. Furthermore, the baby's eyes were wide open, and she was smiling as if greeting them. Undoubtedly, she was a beautiful child. Her skin was a rich burnt sienna color; her eyes were large and dark with a penetrating look to them, and her hair was silky jet black.

Instantly, the word began to spread around the village about the extraordinary baby. People began gathering at the house to catch a glimpse of the baby with the white glowing light.

One by one, the villagers approached the humble house. Each one noticed that the light was emanating from the baby's chest area, which they called the heart chakra. Although they were not sure what it meant, they concluded that the baby was special. They began praying and giving thanks to God for the gift that was bestowed upon the family and their village.

Suddenly, a visitor appeared in the midst of all the excitement. No one had ever seen him before. Even though he was dressed like the villagers and spoke their language, there was something peculiar about the man that they could not figure out. As he moved to the front of the crowd, they felt a divine presence among them. The villagers contemplated the stranger in profound wonder. Then, the stranger spoke, and everyone remained silent.

"God has heeded the prayers of His children on Earth. He has sent this shining star to assist all those who are in need of spiritual light and guidance so they can evolve spiritually. She will take your suffering, worries, and pain and make them her own. She has come to Earth to save souls and remove them from the darkness. She will help you to eradicate the seeds of evil from your souls and replenish it with love.

"After today, the memory of this divine revelation will be expunged from your minds. Although you will not recall anything, your souls will feel as if you have been submerged in a sea of love. God has blessed you all. Go back to your homes and praise God for He has not forgotten you," the visitor revealed.

The man then walked into the crowd and vanished. Instantly, the crowd began to disperse. They moved as if in a trance of some sort. As they walked home, the sound of prayer and song praising God was heard. The following day, everything was back to normal. No one remembered the visitor or the occurrences of the day before. The light encircling the baby was no longer visible.

Tara, the name her parents had given her, was born into a family that was poverty-stricken. When things went from bleak to bleaker, the family always managed to preserve a good disposition. Although they lacked many material items, there was always an abundance of love in their home.

From the beginning, Tara was viewed by the villagers as being unique. She was not like other children who liked to play games or spend time with children of similar age. She preferred the solitude of the fields where she would spend hours meditating.

Tara was approximately five years old when she first wandered off into the fields to meditate. Not knowing where she had gone, her parents became frantic and searched for her everywhere. After looking all over, without much success, Aditya suggested going to the fields. In the middle of nowhere, they found Tara sitting in a lotus position, with her eyes closed and a smile on her face. There was such a pristine look about her that Aditya and Maya dared not interrupt her. Unexpectedly, Tara opened her eyes and faced her parents.

"How dare you walk away without telling anybody. We have been looking for you for hours. I thought something awful had happened to you. I was worried sick!" her mother exclaimed.

With a smile on her face, Tara got up, walked over to her mother, and hugged her thigh.

"Why were you frightened? I was with God. He will always protect me," she said.

Immediately, her mother felt a bolt of calmness shoot down her body; she hugged and kissed Tara.

The words of Tara brought tears to Aditya's eyes. He lifted Tara and kissed her. As they walked away, they knew that their child was special.

Whenever Tara disappeared, they knew exactly where to find her. She would be in the middle of the field in a state of spiritual ecstasy.

Down the road lived a family of much better means than Tara's family. Aala, the wife, was calling her oldest son, Akeem.

"Akeem, go quickly and fetch Bandu. Your father is getting worse."

Aala's husband, Aamir, had been sick for two weeks, and was not getting better. She wanted Bandu, the village's herbalist, to check him out.

Bandu arrived and went to work immediately. After checking Aamir's tongue, eyes, and pulse, he began jotting down some notes.

"Your husband seems to be suffering from a stomach virus. I am prescribing several herbs to be given three times a day. Here are the instructions on how to prepare the herbals. I will return by the end of the week," he told Aala.

The family faithfully administered the herbs as directed by Bandu. By the end of the week, there was no visible improvement. His condition continued to worsen.

Aala was sweeping the front entrance when Bandu arrived.

"Greeting, Aala. How is Aamir today?" Bandu stated.

Aala lowered her head and said, "Aamir is not well."

Bandu noticed that her eyes were red and filled with tears. She had been crying all morning.

Aala put the broom down and escorted Bandu to Aamir's room. Aamir was in bed with his eyes closed. He was pale and emaciated.

"Aamir, can you hear me?" asked Bandu.

Aamir opened his eyes slowly. With much effort, he said, "Yes."

Bandu was perplexed. He rubbed his forehead and stared at Aamir as if trying to come up with another solution. He believed that Aamir was suffering from a stomach virus, and the prescribed herbs should have addressed the problem.

"Did you follow my instructions?" he asked Aala

"Yes, we did everything according to your directions. But he has no appetite and is too weak to get out of bed," Aala replied.

Bandu sighed and shook his head as he examined Aamir. Once again, Bandu prescribed a stronger batch of herbs.

"These herbs should resolve the problem. Make sure he eats something because these herbs are strong. No solid foods. I'll be back in a few days," he said.

Two days later, Bandu arrived to check on Aamir. Once again, he was baffled. His mind was racing, searching for answers to Aamir's problem. However, he could not think of anything else to give him.

Aamir was losing weight rapidly and could no longer sit or talk. The herbs had not produced any favorable results.

"I have given him the strongest herbs, and it has not helped. There is nothing more I can do. The best thing is to consult a medical doctor," Bandu suggested.

Since the village did not have a doctor, Akeem traveled to the next village. The doctor agreed to visit his father. When the doctor arrived, Aamir appeared to be in a semi-conscious state. He was extremely fragile and thin. The doctor examined Aamir, took some blood, and wrote a prescription.

"Your husband is suffering from a stomach ailment that appears to have been complicated by his lack of nourishment. This medication will correct the problem. There is nothing to worry about. I will return by the end of the week," he said.

Akeem traveled quickly to the next village to attain the prescribed medication. For the entire week, the medication was given as directed by the doctor. However, the situation had reached a critical state. Aamir's immune system seemed to be shutting down. Frequently, he experienced coughing attacks and shortness of breath. During these attacks, he would discharge an abundance of mucus mixed with blood. He was no longer eating or speaking. The family feared the worst.

The blood test results revealed a rare blood disease. Although the doctor wanted to do more tests, his resources were limited.

A few days later, the doctor arrived. He immediately checked Aamir's vital signs. His pulse was extremely weak. The overall picture was not good. He gathered the family in the next room and informed them of the test results. Although he had no particulars on the rare blood disorder, he knew for sure that Aamir was dying. His body was shutting down slowly. He advised them to prepare for the unavoidable.

"In my professional opinion, I believe he only has a few days left. His vital signs are all extremely poor," he stated.

Aala fell to the ground. Tears began gushing from her grieving eyes.

"My husband is leaving me. What am I going to do without him?" she said with a trembling voice.

Akeem and his siblings rushed to their mother's side.

With tears in his eyes, Akeem addressed the family. "We need to have courage."

The next day, they decided to make the necessary funeral arrangements. Death was inevitable.

Two days later, the family had gathered to pray while Aamir was in the adjacent room. Suddenly, they heard voices coming from his room. They looked at each other and simultaneously said, "What is that?" They got up quickly and rush to Aamir's room. When they walked in, they saw Tara and Aamir talking and laughing. Aamir got up suddenly and said, "Can I get something to eat? I am starving."

The family looked at each other in complete astonishment. They could not believe what they were seeing and hearing. Aamir, who was on his deathbed, was now talking, laughing and standing. He even wanted something to eat. Overcome by indefinable joy, and with tears in their eyes, they rushed to his side and began hugging and kissing him. They were so excited that no one noticed that Tara had disappeared.

Aala turned around and with much joy in her voice said, "Tara, how did you get here? Tara, where are you? Where is Tara?" They looked around the house and backyard, but could not find her. They rushed to Tara's house to see if she had gone home.

Maya heard a knock on the door. She and Aditya got up and opened the door. It was the family from down the road.

"Yes, how can we help you?" Aditya said.

"Forgive us for this late hour visit, but we want to know if Tara is here. She was at our house and disappeared suddenly," Aala said.

"Tara was at your house? You are mistaken. Tara has been sleeping for hours. Come in and see for yourself," Maya said.

When they approached Tara, she was sound asleep.

"This cannot be. We all saw her talking and laughing with our father," replied Akeem.

Aamir spoke, "I was in bed unable to move with my eyes closed. Pain had spread over all my body. I could not bear it any longer. I knew that death was near. I was barely breathing. I was praying to God to take me away as soon as possible. When I opened my eyes, Tara was sitting on the bed next to me. At first, I was stunned, but promptly felt an indescribable feeling of calmness. She spoke to me with immense love and caring. It reminded me of when I was a child and my mother would speak to me in a loving way. Tara told me that God wanted me to get up from bed for there was much for me to do in this lifetime. It was not my time to meet the celestial angels. Then she held my hands. I felt a bolt of current traveling all over my body. It was as if God had blown new life into my dying body. Suddenly, I was sitting up, talking and laughing. But, how can this be? She is fast asleep."

Aamir, feeling moved by the presence of Tara, wept and kneeled next to Tara. He began praying and giving thanks. In minutes, the two families had joined to pray.

The following day, a goat and a large basket with fruits, vegetables, and rice were left in front of Tara's house.

Tara continued to develop her gift of bilocation- the ability to be in two places simultaneously. During meditation, she would leave her body and visit distant villages. People would see her in the flesh, preaching and healing the sick.

One day, a man arrived at the village. He had been traveling for days searching for Tara. She had told him to come to her village for further healing. He had been bedridden and suffering from an incurable disease when Tara appeared in his home.

"I am Tara," she said, as she approached him.

Although the house was empty and she appeared out of nowhere, he was not frightened. In fact, he felt immense inner peace.

She smiled and placed her hand on his forehead. She then closed her eyes and whispered a few words as if speaking to some invisible force. An intense spark entered his body leaving him mobile and energized.

"Come to my village for further healing," were the last words she said before disappearing.

A day later, he went to see his doctor. The doctor was surprised to see him moving around. After a series of tests, the doctor was perplexed by his findings.

"How can this be? The cancerous tumors are no longer present. Even your symptoms have disappeared. You are completely cured," the doctor said, with a tone of amazement in his voice.

The stranger did not reveal the visit from Tara.

Although he was ignorant of the location of Tara's village, he felt a mysterious force guiding his footsteps. After a week of traveling by foot, he reached his destination. He immediately felt he was in the right place when he entered the village. His heart started racing and tears began flowing down his face.

"Excuse me. Can you help me? Is there a young girl by the name of

Tara living in this village? She had visited my village and told me to come to her village for further healing," he told the villager.

"Yes, Tara lives here. But, are you sure it is Tara you are looking for? Tara has never left the village. I will take you to her," the villager responded.

When the stranger saw Tara, he bowed his head. Tara greeted him with a smile. It was as if she knew he was coming. The place was empty. She directed him to a seat nearby.

With much tenderness, she spoke. "Why is your heart so empty? Why have you allowed your soul to be adsorbed by darkness? Although your body is healed, the soul is not. For so long, you have prevented love from entering your heart. Love is a gift from God. It is the cure that allows the soul to be whole. Without Love, the soul is meaningless drifting in obscurity ."

Tears began flowing down his face. He understood the message fully. For many years, he had carried much hate and anger inside him. He could not accept his illness and blamed God for his situation. When family and friends offered to assist him, he would release his anger and hate upon them. For countless years, he lived a life in darkness and isolation.

"Those are tears of celebration. Today, you will be reborn," she continued. She grabbed his hands and closed her eyes. She began speaking a few words to herself. The stranger bowed his head and closed his eyes. Instantly, an inexplicable feeling of adoration overtook him. His heart began racing and body vibrating. When he opened his eyes, he was in profound wonderment. He saw Tara dressed in a majestic white robe covered by a luminous golden light. Behind her were several radiant beings dressed in white. Although he could not comprehend fully what was happening, he knew that a divine intervention was taking place. Instinctively, he got on his knees and prayed. He wept uncontrollably. When he got up, Tara was no longer around. He sat down and continued to pray. A few hours later, the place was crowded with people and Tara was in the front of the room attending lovely each individual.

From that moment, the stranger became Tara's most devoted follower and made Tara's village his permanent home. He remained cancer-free and spread the word of love to all those who were willing to listen.

News of Tara's spiritual abilities began to spread rapidly. People from distant lands began arriving at her village in search of physical, emotional and spiritual healing. The relatively small village was swarmed with outsiders. In order to maintain the stability of their village, the villagers built a substantial size hut on the outskirts of the village. There, Tara lovingly attended to the needs of the multitude that arrived each day. She would hold their hands, lower her head, and close her eyes. Then, she would whisper a few words. Although no one saw anyone around her, the people she treated sensed a spiritual presence next to her.

One woman, who was treated by Tara, said the following, "My daughter took me to see Tara. I had been ill for numerous years with debilitating arthritis that kept me immobile and wheelchair bound. This young, sweet girl grabbed my hand and began whispering a few words as if speaking to someone. When Tara proceeded to heal me, I closed my eyes and prayed to God. Immediately, I felt something like an electrical current going up and down my body. When I opened my eyes, I saw a blinding white light covering Tara's entire body. Thinking there was something wrong with my eyes, I blinked several times. I was astounded. Then, I heard her say, 'You can go now.' I quickly got up and walked away. When I turned around, the luminous light was still there. I approached my daughter, who was sitting nearby, and asked her, 'Did you see the light?' In a tone of extreme emotion and teary eyes, she said, 'You are walking.' At that moment, I realized I was walking unassisted and pain free. It was a true miracle. Now, I no longer use a wheelchair; I am active in the full sense of the word. I will never forget that experience. It will forever remain fixed in my memory."

One day, a lady who had come to the village to seek healing, said to Tara, "Whom are you speaking to? I don't see anyone, but I sense something around you."

Tara smiled and said, "I can't do this alone. I am just an instrument. There are many of God's invisible healers here."

Although Tara had attained very little educational schooling, men of high religious orders were stunned by the spiritual knowledge she possessed. Tara easily explained complex spiritual questions that perplexed the minds of the most respected religious scholars. It was said that the knowledge she possessed came directly from God.

Meanwhile, a few miles away, a terrorist group had set up a training camp. Their mission was to infiltrate and recruit young men from the surrounding villages. They presented themselves as holy men proclaiming to be the messengers of God.

"It is written that Allah will punish those who refuse to adhere to His divine laws. Infidels will be hunted down and destroyed. Let us become Allah's earthly soldiers and wipe clean the Earth of undesirables. For it is Allah's holy will. Let us praise Allah and offer our services and devotion to Him. Praise Allah now and always for He is great," they preached.

When they approached the villagers from the near-by villages, the villagers' demeanors did not please them. The villagers believed it was their duty to help and love their fellow man, instead of harming them. They spoke of forgiving his enemies and doing good deeds. This was not what the extremists expected. The minds of the villagers could not be corrupted.

They discovered that not far from their campsite lived a young woman who was responsible for villagers' manner of thinking. Her name was Tara, and she needed to be stopped. When the men informed their commander of what had transpired, he ordered his men to abduct the woman and bring her to him. He had a mission to fulfill, and no one was going to interfere with his plans. If necessary, he would put an end to Tara's life.

Maya was sewing when she heard a knock on the door. She got up to open the door. It was a man inquiring about the whereabouts of Tara.

"Excuse me," said the stranger, "does Tara live here? I wish to see her. My mother is gravely ill, and I was told that Tara possesses healing power."

"Tara is not here. She is meditating. If you walk straight ahead, you will see a hut. She sees people there. Take your mother there. She will be there in an hour or two," Maya said amicably.

The man thanked her and walked away.

For two days, the man followed Tara learning her daily routine. By six o'clock in the morning, she was on her way to the fields. She remained there isolated and in deep meditation for several hours. It was the perfect opportunity to abduct her.

Tara was heading to the fields to meditate when a stranger approached her.

"Hello, are you lost?" she asked politely.

The man smiled and replied, "I am not lost. This is where I need to be."

Grabbing her arm, he pulled her towards him. He gagged and bounded her hands. Tara did not struggle or cry for help. It was as if she knew what was about to happen. Another man appeared in an old beat up car. They threw her inside and drove away.

When they arrived at the campsite, several men had gathered around. They were eager to see the woman who was responsible for convincing villagers to love everyone regardless of their religious beliefs.

Suddenly, the commander appeared. He greeted Tara with much disdain.

"So, you are the one who has been preaching a lot of nonsense," he said.

After staring at Tara for a few minutes, he ordered one of his men to tie her to a tree.

"Leave her there without water or food until I decide her fate."

Meanwhile, the villagers searched frantically for Tara, but to no avail. They could not understand why she disappeared.

For two days, Tara was strapped to a tree without food or water. The ropes had caused her hands to swell due to the lack of circulation. The burning sun and lack of water produced sores around her lips. The stench of human waste contaminated the air. It was the commander's method of humiliating her. However, Tara never complained. She kept her eyes closed and remained in a meditative state.

Some men passed by her and laughed while others spit and insulted her. One man pulled out his genital and urinated in front of her, yelling,

"Do you want some of this, witch?" Everyone broke out in laughter. Tara's composure was serene throughout the entire ordeal.

"Bring me the prisoner," the commander ordered one of his men.

Soiled, battered, and frail, Tara was dragged to the main tent where the commander and numerous men were waiting. There was silence as Tara was flung to the ground in front of the commander.

"A hearing has been arranged to determine your fate," the commander uttered.

"You are accused of being a witch and using sorcery to twist and corrupt the minds of the people. I am giving you a chance to repent and retract your teachings. Confess your sins."

Tara raised her head and looked directly into the commander's eyes. As if inspired by a divine power, she began to speak without hesitation or fear, "I serve God. However, you call me a witch and sorceress. If teaching people to love one another and healing the sick are works of sorcery, then I am guilty of being a witch. My inspiration comes from God. Spreading love and healing the sick derive from God. He wants His children to know that love is the key to true happiness. How can you sit there and claim to be doing God's work when you are destroying everything He has created? Right this minute, God is here. He is not here to praise you for your work. He is here to witness your madness. A powerful evil force is manipulating your thoughts and actions. You are not the cure. You are the disease. Your immense hate for humanity has blocked God's love from entering your heart. You need to ask God for forgiveness and allow His love to enter your soul."

The commander rudely interrupted Tara. Possessed by immense fury, he proceeded to shout. "You have talked enough. Since you will not confess to anything, I sentence you to die by fire as soon as possible."

After hearing the death penalty, there was uproar in the tent. The men chanted fiercely and continuously, "Burn the witch- a Satan worshipper."

It was midday when Tara was moved to the center of the campsite. There, she was ruthlessly tied to a post that was cemented into the ground. Beneath her feet were large pieces of wood spread around the post. The commander sat waiting for the right moment to commence the execution.

Meanwhile, a large group of men had gathered to witness the burning of Tara. They were silent when the commander spoke.

With a cynical look on his face, the commander once again addressed Tara. "Admit that you are a witch and use sorcery. Also, a devil worshipper. This is your last opportunity to save yourself."

"I am a messenger of God doing His work. You can destroy my body, but my soul belongs to God and it will never die," Tara replied.

"Enough! Death to the witch!" the commander shouted furiously.

The commander, with a lit torch, walked quickly towards Tara. With much eagerness, he threw the torch into the pile of wood that was beneath Tara's feet. With an odious look in his eyes, he exclaimed, "Now, you will die!"

The flames quickly spread around the area where Tara stood. In no time, the fire had worked itself up to Tara's legs. The smell of burning flesh was stomach-churning. However, the commander and his men rejoiced without showing any signs of disgust or compassion.

Cheering the brutal act of the commander, the crowd hollered, "Death to the devil worshipper."

Tara graciously smiled and closed her eyes. As the fire began consuming Tara's delicate body and the air was filled with the stench of burnt flesh, laughter and obscenities filled the air.

"Burn, witch, burn!" the men chanted.

The commander sat relishing the moment. He felt that the act would secure his fate as the true messenger of Allah.

Suddenly, the laughter and shouting ceased. The sky had turned dark; and an image emerged from the flames. It was the image of a woman with a powerful luminous light encasing her body.

"It's Tara!" shouted one of the men.

Although Tara's body was utterly scorched, her spirit lived on.

Immediately, the commander stood up. His eyes and mouth were wide opened. He could not believe what he was observing.

Then, a voice from within the light said, "You cannot kill that which is eternal."

The Commander, infuriated by the spoken words, pulled out his machete from the side of his belt. Lunging towards Tara's spirit, he exclaimed, "You will definitely die. Death to the sorcerer!"

Upon swinging the machete, his entire body became paralyzed. He fell to the ground incapable of moving. Not only was his body incapacitated, he lost the ability to speak or see. Tears streamed from his eyes. The powerful looking commander became impotent. While attempting to destroy Tara, the commander sealed his own fate.

The divine figure moved closer to the commander. She reached out and grabbed his hand. Upon touching him, the commander's body began to respond. He kneeled and wept even more profusely. Although his speech returned, his sight did not. He begged God for forgiveness.

"Oh, dear Allah, please forgive me for I now know what greatness means. Because of my thirst for power, I was blinded and could not see the purity and greatness of this young girl. She is your true messenger. I beg you to forgive me," he declared in a humble and emotional tone.

After witnessing the incident, many of the men ran away while others kneeled and begged for forgiveness and mercy.

The fire continued to gain momentum. It had reached a peak where neighboring villagers were able to witness the immensity of the blaze. As if prompted by an invisible force, villagers began gravitating towards the area of illumination caused by the flame. When they reached the vicinity of the fire, they were in awe when they saw a penetrating bright light in the form of a woman kneeling and praying in front of the fire. Instantly, the large crowd kneeled and prayed.

Not long before the group had begun to pray, the divine figure stood up and addressed the crowd. After seeing her closely, many recognized her.

"It's Tara!," they whispered among themselves.

"Yes, I was Tara. I am no longer she for I have taken my true form. I am one of God's messengers. My mission on Earth was to spread God's love to all His children. He wants everyone to know that without love, you are hollow souls roaming the Earth aimlessly. Love is the cure to all emotional and spiritual ills. In order to receive love, you must give love. Love is not something you just say; it is something you feel deep inside. In order for love to grow, it needs to be nurtured. What difference does it make if you are from a different caste, race, religion, or social or educational status? The purpose of the soul is to evolve to a higher spiritual level. However, this can only be accomplished by showing compassion and loving one another. Hate only creates more hate; and killing only produces more killing. Instead of moving forward, these negative acts will keep you confined to a sea of darkness. Remember, you are all God's children. Do good deeds to self and others. God will be waiting for you in His kingdom."

Deeply moved by Tara's words, many in the crowd began sobbing while others lowered their heads and prayed silently in gratitude.

"Take the ashes of my body and share it with others. Where there is hate, may my ashes generate love; where there is sickness, may my ashes generate health; where there is hopelessness, may my ashes generate hope and faith; and where there are destructive thoughts, may my ashes generate love, peace and light," Tara said lovingly.

Tara moved towards the commander, who had been weeping and praying non-stop, and placed her hands on his eyes. Feeling a burning sensation, the commander rubbed his eyes. Gradually, images began to appear until his eyesight was fully restored.

Tara returned to the fire and walked in, disappearing immediately. The fire began to subside. On top of Tara's scorched and lifeless body, a bright shining star appeared. It began moving upward slowly until it was no longer visible.

Meanwhile, the people began faithfully collecting the ashes. As they walked away toward their respective homes, the sound of prayer and song praising God was heard. It was the same sound that was heard on the day the stranger appeared during the birth of Tara.

The commander disappeared among the crowd never to be heard of again.

Many people believe that Tara's spirit continues to visit the homes of those suffering physically, emotionally, and spiritually, taking away their pain and filling their hearts with love. They say that whenever you see a flicker of light flashing in front of your eyes, it is Tara paying you a visit. She comes to bring blessings into your home. Although her flesh does not exist, her spirit lives on.

CHAPTER 7

BATOLO-SPIRIT GUIDE

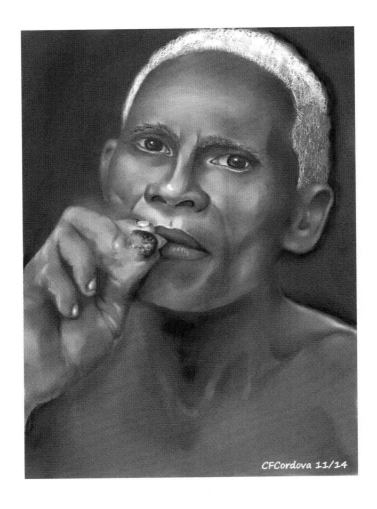

CFCordova 11/14

It was 1 pm when the spiritual gathering commenced. A small group of mediums was sitting in a circle. In the center was a moderately sized table with a candle, a crystal, a cross, and a goblet filled with water on top. One of the mediums began reading from an Allan Kardec book called *The Gospel According to Spiritism*. After the reading, a brief discussion was conducted followed by prayers. When the prayers ended, the mediums closed their eyes and meditated while soft spiritual music played in the background. After a while, one of the mediums began jerking and shivering in her seat. With her eyes closed and leaning forward, the medium began to speak.

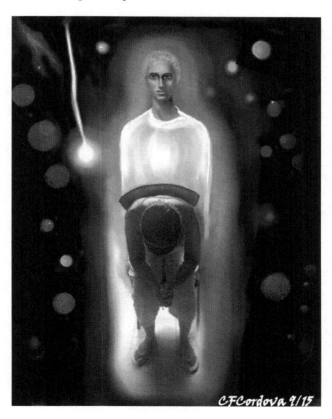

"May the peace of God be here. May Olofi (personification of the divine) be here." Then, the medium knocked three times on the floor.

Although the words were coming out of the medium's mouth, the mannerisms and behavior were definitely not hers. It was one of the medium's spirit guides called Batolo. He had taken over the body in order to communicate with the group.

After greeting the group, the spirit requested a cigar.

The medium, under the influence of the entity, placed the lit portion of the cigar inside her mouth. The medium puffed on the cigar once or twice allowing the smoke to interlink with the energy already in the room. It was a purification ritual of some sort.

"How are the people here doing today?" the spirit asked joyfully in a thick accent.

"Fine," responded the group.

"Does anyone have any questions?"

There was silence. Then, a group member spoke.

"Yes, I have a question. Can you tell us how you became a spirit guide?"

After a brief pause, Batolo replied.

"Why do you want to know?"

"You are such an interesting energy that I just want to know more," the person said.

This time, the pause was a bit longer. The group remained silent waiting for Batolo's response.

"Right now, I am not permitted to answer your question. In time, if I am given permission, I will reveal the details to the instrument and she will share it with you."

After interacting with the group in a loving and jovial way, Batolo said his goodbyes and departed.

"Never do harm to anyone with your actions or thoughts. The harm you do to others will return to you tenfold," were Batolo last words.

Several weeks later, the medium was meditating. Instantly, she entered a semi-dream state. She heard a voice speaking to her. It was Batolo. Through her third eye, she saw a bare-chested, older, dark man with a pleasant smile. He began communicating with her telepathically. It was the beginning of a captivating narrative.

"Hello. You know me as Batolo. I am here to share some information about self and spirit world. I will begin with my last incarnation and conclude with my present mission.

"My last incarnation was an eon ago in a land now known as Africa. It was a time when the land was not contaminated or covered with the blood and tears of its inhabitants. Rather, it was a time when we communicated and lived in harmony with nature. The land was pure and as God intended. It was for the enjoyment of all God's children. The pureness of the land was definitely a paradise on Earth. We respected all of God's creations. What we took from nature was for the sole purpose of survival, and not for destructive means.

"My village was located in the mountains. Many of God's magnificent work of art surrounded us.. There were beautiful waterfalls, trees, animals, and much more. We saw God in each piece of His artwork. We called God, 'He who lives above.' We believed that God had many spirit helpers who remained on earth to protect the land. Each one was responsible for a particular aspect of the land. Whenever we took from the land, we thanked God and then His helpers.

"The village consisted of various families. The houses were constructed of wood and strong vines. They were so well made that they protected us from the Earth elements. Although there were numerous families, we considered ourselves as one, everyone helping each other altruistically.

"My mother died giving birth to me. She gave up her life in order for me to come into the world. Although I did not have my biological mother, the women of my village provided me with motherly love.

"The women of the village were regarded as special beings and held in high esteem. They were God's special creations. They were the instruments God used to bring humans into the world. Without them, humanity would not exist.

"My grandfather was the village's medicine man or healer. My father was trained in the numerous facets of healing. Although he showed aptitude, he lacked passion. He did not continue to the final stage- initiation. He preferred hunting. It was his true passion.

"I was the opposite of my father. Healing was my passion. Apart from learning the various aspects of survival, the secrets or mysteries of the spirit world were a paramount part of my schooling. My grandfather saw me as a gifted healer. He taught me everything he knew. From a young age, the diverse aspects of healing enthralled me. Spirits were the primary attribute. In order to perform healing rituals, the healer needed to establish a strong connection with spirits and become the vehicle in which they worked.

"My fondest memories of that lifetime were my trips to the forest with my grandfather. We would stay in the forest for days collecting herbs and performing rituals. He taught me about the healing properties of each plant, flower, tree bark, and, most of all, the connection between the universe and us. I remember him telling me, 'Respect and love all things for they are precious gifts from the one that lives above. Remember, just because you don't see something doesn't mean it doesn't exist.' His last statement was referring to spirits.

"The nights were magical. We slept under trees admiring the star-filled night sky. My grandfather would point to the sky and say, 'That's where the spirit helpers come from. Spirit helpers have been around from the very beginning. They were sent here to help us and protect the planet.'

"From early on, I began seeing and communicating with spirits. My grandfather said I had the gift of sight. At first, they presented themselves as a misty cloud. However, as I got accustomed to the images, they began to take a much more recognizable form. One of the figures was of a tall elderly man dressed in a white robe. He said that he was sent from above to guide me during my lifetime on Earth. He remained by my side throughout my stay here. Even though there were other spirit friends that would come from time to time, my elderly spirit friend was always close-by.

"Although I was not a rich man in terms of material wealth and I did not possess a scholarly education, I was blessed with an abundance of spiritual richness and comprehension.

"When I reached a certain age, my grandfather took me to the forest for my initiation ritual. My grandfather, along with certain village members, performed my initiation to become a healer. It was near a waterfall that we believed had spiritual energy. Each process started with the calling to God and His spirit helpers. The initiation consisted of fasting, cleansing with different spiritually charged herbs, bathing in the waterfall several times, chanting, and more. After a couple of days, I was left alone in the forest. There I chanted consistently and connected with spirits. I became one with the energy of the forest. At the end of the initiation phase, my grandfather and two other village members came and took me home. I was considered a healer and my grandfather's assistant.

"I became extremely skillful in the healing practices. My grandfather opened the door and introduced me to the world of healing while my spirit friends guided me every step of the way.

"When my grandfather passed away, I became the village healer. I was quite proficient in the field; people from other villages would travel to our village to attain healing. My entire life was devoted to healing and doing God's work. Healing was not only of the physical and mental, it encompassed the soul. In fact, in numerous cases, the person's demons were attached to the deep level of the person's soul. When the soul was healed, the physical and/or mental levels of the person became healthy.

"As a custom of the village, I married young. It was an arranged marriage. I became a widower at a young age. My elderly spirit friend foretold of my wife's demise. There was nothing I could do. It was her time to journey back home. I never remarried. Although I had no blood children, I was the father of many. The village children were my children. As mentioned previously, the village was like one big family.

"I lived to be an old man. In my last moments on earth, loving faces surrounded me. I was truly blessed to have loving people around me.

"As I took my last breath, my spirit slowly detached itself from the body. I was no longer a tired old man. I had returned to my true being, which was completely different from my earthly body. I was younger with diverse features. After separating from the body, departed relatives and spirit guides surrounded me. They remained by my side as I watched the ceremony performed by the village members for the departure of my soul. When the ceremony was concluded, my elderly spirit friend accompanied me on my journey.

"We entered a powerful white light that was in front of us and continued moving forward. It felt like a potent force was guiding us along the way. There was no time to think about anything. We continued moving until we reached a high mountaintop in the spirit realm. The place was quite familiar to me but, at the moment, I could not remember details. Memories felt jumbled and fragmented.

"My friend told me that the place was called the purification center. It was the first stage of the spirit's transition. This place was where newly arrived souls entered to begin the process of purging all remaining residues from the previous life on earth. When I entered the center, my spirit friend remained outside. He smiled and walked away. His mission had ended for now.

"The inside of the purification center was vast with several large rooms. The majority of the rooms were used for healing. Each room contained many resting apparatuses, which you would refer to as beds. A spirit assistant directed me to lie down on one of the beds. Soon, other spirit assistants appeared. They placed their hands above me. They began extracting earthly emotions and thoughts that were no longer needed. A murky mist emanated out of my spirit moving slowly upward and disappearing gradually. They continued to maintain their hands extended creating a magnetic field around me. The entire process was conducted in complete silence.

At some point, I felt into a deep sleep. The process consists of extracting, resting and recovering. When I woke up, my earthly memories were a distant remembrance that was no longer linked to me.

"Not all spirits go through this process. Those that avoid entering the light are referred to as lost souls or ghosts who remain stuck to the Earth atmosphere. They remain in a realm of darkness caused by their negative deeds or thoughts. Although they have the ability to free themselves from the darkness and enter the light, many refuse to do so. They become captives of their own negative energy.

"It is important to remember that all souls have free will and can enter the light of God whenever they wish to let go of all negative energies and seek healing.

"Since the concept of time, as you know it, is non-existent in the spirit world, I do not know how long I was in the healing center. Throughout the time I was there, I received constant healing and guidance from the spirit assistants.

"When the process was completed, I was reunited with my relatives and friends. Although many of my relatives and friends were not a part of my last incarnation, I knew them well and was elated to see them. It was like a homecoming. When I did not see my father from my previous life, I was told he had returned to Earth to confront and resolve some personal soul issues.

"My grandfather from my last incarnation was not a part of the gathering. He had ascended to a higher celestial realm. From time to time, he would come to visit. He was very different from the earthly figure of his last incarnation. He was tall with distinct features and a balsamic glow around him. I always had a pure love for him. His soul, whether incarnate or discarnate, continuously guided me through my numerous earthly trials.

"Our souls were linked together. On many instances, we shared the same lifetime assisting each other to advance spiritually. In one incarnation, he was my older brother who protected and guided me. It is true what they say about souls traveling together for diverse reasons.

"It is important to keep in mind that during your earthly journey, you will meet many incarnate souls. Some will be of your liking while others will not. Always be alert and open to these brief or long-lasting encounters, for it is possible that they bring valuable lessons for you to learn from.

"Every day, I attended the temple of prayer. The temple was shaped as a triangle. The inside consisted of a large empty space with a high ceiling. In the center of the ceiling was an opening in which a potent, brilliant light filtered through. The atmosphere inside was highly charged with divine energy. From time to time, sparkling stars would come down from the opening of the ceiling, detach themselves from the light, and roam above us. They were highly evolved spirits who gathered around to provide healing energy.

"There was always a group present praying or in deep meditation. They sat on the floor with their eyes closed facing the light. They prayed for incarnate as well as discarnate souls who were lingering aimlessly. Sometimes, a distant sound of a ringing bell was heard. It was a signal alerting the group in attendance that another group would be coming in. If you wanted to stay, you were welcome to do so. Since newly arrived souls were in the healing process, they were encouraged to stay as long as needed. I took advantage of the opportunity.

"When my soul was fully cleansed of all earthly attachments and emotions, I was allowed to view all of my lifetimes and measure my spiritual progress. This took place in another building called The Place of Records. This is the place where all of the soul's good and bad deeds from all lifetimes are stored. These records provide information on the soul's advancement and/or what is lacking for soul improvement. The main purpose of these records is to offer guidance to the soul in order to achieve a higher level of enlightenment.

"In the spirit realm, spirits are encouraged to work and train for the betterment of all souls. One day, I received a notification. I was selected to undergo training. I was given the choice to accept or reject the offer. I accepted the opportunity. Many, incarnate as well as discarnate souls, are oblivious that free will is one of the greatest gifts God has given us.

"I was told that my openness, acceptance, and willingness to work with spirits during my last incarnation abetted my soul to acquire a higher level of spiritual enlightenment. It was one of the main reasons I was chosen for spirit guide training.

"I was one of many who were called for spirit guide training. Although it mainly consisted of learning to establish a higher level of communication with incarnate souls and becoming acquainted with the different functions of spirit guides, the experience was profound. A major precept of spirit guide work was that spirits could make suggestions to individuals, but not impose them. Spirit guides must comply with the concept of free will. There were three groups of spirit guides. One group, called direct guidance, was assigned to individuals; another group roamed the planet Earth assisting those in need; and the last group remained at the gates of earth on standby or ready to assist the planet when major catastrophe occurred. I was designated to the direct guidance group. Each group had one senior. The senior's job was to drop off novice spirit guides to their destination.

"Upon arrival to the earth realm, I was taken to a hospital by the senior. He pointed to a mother who was about to give birth. The mother was pushing hard while the doctor assisted her. I was appointed the spirit guide of the unborn child. The unborn child was you. There were numerous spirits of light surrounding your mother and you. They were spirit guides and relatives of both you and your mother. I was an observer witnessing the work of the spirits of light. They had created a powerful protecting shield around you and your mother to ward off impure spirits that were roaming the room. Since your mother was a medium and you were destined for spiritual mediumship, it was essential to keep impure energy at bay.

"Although I was appointed to be your spirit guide, numerous spirit guides were also assigned to you. As mentioned before, you were destined to become a medium.

"In addition to the spirit guides, there was one principal guide. This guide was above all of us and had an extensive history with your incarnate spirit. It had been your spirit guide during other lifetimes.

"I, as well as other guides, remained vigilant of all of your activities throughout your growing years. We were not allowed to interfere in your spiritual developmental process for there were essential trials you needed to experience.

"My training continued. I was learning more and more from higher advance spirits who were constantly monitoring your development. My goal was to observe and assist in providing positive energy.

"Your childhood years were quite interesting. Although part of you was aware of our existence nearby, another part experienced fear. The panic became evident in the nighttime when one of the spirits would manifest in front of you. During these moments, you screamed and cried uncontrollably.

"Many humans are taught to fear the unknown or not believe in what they can't see. Therefore, when they have a spiritual encounter they chalk it off to coincidence, hallucinations, or a mental abnormality. However, children's minds operate in a simplistic mode. They react accordingly to what they see or feel. If they are frightened, they cry, if they are happy, they smile, and so on. Their thoughts are pure and not contaminated with analytical thinking. This is the reason why it is easier for children to communicate with spirits.

"As you continued to develop physically and mentally, your spiritual abilities were also emerging. The spiritual fluid like substance that makes it possible for mediums to incorporate spirits was becoming sturdier. The visible eye does not see this substance. It is strictly spiritual. I refer to it as a pathway in which the spirit enters to connect with the medium's spiritual senses. As mediums develop their mediumship, maintain it pure, remain humble and perform good deeds, the pathway continues to expand, providing a more profound spiritual experience.

"On the other hand, mediums who possess greedy, evil, and egotistical ways tend to create pathways which are narrow with a dark grayish color substance. They tend to attract spirits of darkness, which eventually wreaks havoc in the lives of the mediums as well as those seeking spiritual help. Therefore, it is vital that mediums maintain a high level of humility.

"You were extremely young when you began incorporating spiritual energy. For a long time, I remained in the background observing and learning. My role was to contribute, along with others, spiritual energy whenever it was needed.

"Each time you engaged in spiritual work, all of the spirit guides came together and created a powerful energy force. The energy force was for your protection as well as the recipient against negative and harmful forces. Although one spirit was allowed to incorporate the body at a time, it was the energy of many spirits of light that produced the end results.

"Then, one day, I was given the opportunity to enter the pathway and bond with your senses. My energy, as well as yours, became one.

'May Olofi be here. May God's peace be here…my name is Batolo,' was my opening message. You remained in a semi-conscious state throughout the communication.

"A semi-conscious state means that the medium is slightly aware of what is happening, but cannot control the situation. She is like the person listening to someone else's conversation without being able to give her opinion. On many occasions, the medium remembers very little of the interaction.

"The more my energy connected with your energy, the easier it got. You became the mouthpiece in which my words came out. At first, the communication was a bit incoherent. In fact, it still is. However, it is improving.

"As you can see, we are still connected. I will remain by your side until you leave your present body. I will continue to communicate with my incarnate brothers and sisters, and work with other spirit guides to help humans connect with God.

"My role is to bring joy and laughter to people while helping them see the true essence of their lives. There is so much sadness and depression roaming the atmosphere that people have forgotten that life is a gift from God to be appreciated and enjoyed. Some have even forgotten how to smile or laugh.

"Furthermore, I strive to assist people to help themselves overcome the many complexities of everyday living, understand his or her life mission and attain a better connection with God.

"Mediums are instruments used to deliver spiritual messages. Although there are different types of mediums —seer, hearer, psychographer, sensitive, incorporative or healer- the goal is the same. They connect with spirits and reveal spiritual truth.   As previously stated, not all mediums are the same. Some pretend to be connected to spirits in order to deceive people and attain monetary gains. They are charlatans who prey on the weak and vulnerable.

"I have been asked if I am an old man. The answer is quite simple. I am neither old nor young. I am energy. I present myself as an old African man because it was my last incarnation where I reached a higher level of spiritual enlightenment. Sometimes, I present myself as a young African man; other times. I appear as a bright light. It does not make a difference. Presenting ourselves in a recognizable human form is to make it easier for the medium to distinguish who is who. For other kinds of mediumship, other means are used.

"It is important to remember never to do harm to yourself as well as others. The harm you do or negative thoughts you send out to others will return to you tenfold. Respect and love God, yourself and others. Love is the key.

"Also, keep in mind, that negative emotions are part of your learning process. Learn from them and let them go. A person who holds on to negative emotions is a prisoner unable to move forward. Cleanse the body and mind, and allow the soul to grow.

"Become the wind that blows the sand; not the sand that waits for the wind to produce some form of change.

"May the peace of God/Olofi be with you."

After the communication, the medium felt a stronger bond with the energy. The energy had become her teacher explaining details of the spirit world.

In the following session, the medium shared the experience with those in attendance. They listened attentively. It was more than what they expected. It had been a captivating story that would live in their minds forever.

CHAPTER 8

WHAT GOES AROUND COMES AROUND

Tom got up and looked at the clock that was near his bed. It was 6 am Saturday morning. He was too anxious to remain in bed. Today, he would compete in the middle school's spelling contest. His two younger brothers were still asleep when he left the room he shared with them. He quietly went to the bathroom, brushed his teeth, and got dressed. When he walked into the kitchen, his father was sitting at the table reading the newspaper while his mother was cooking breakfast.

"You are up early. Are you nervous?" his mother asked.

"A little bit," he replied.

"Don't worry. You will be fine. Sit down and eat your cereal," she said.

Tom sat down and started eating his cereal. His father placed the newspaper down and said, "Your mother told me you will be competing in the school's spelling contest. That's nice. Always remember that the strong will always survive and the weak will perish. You are strong and will always come out on top."

Tom listened attentively.

His father, who was a supervisor in a construction company, was scheduled to work today. As he got up to leave, he said, "Remember what I told you about the strong. Don't worry. You are going to ace it."

Tom smiled and said good-by to his dad.

He finished his cereal quickly and rushed out the door. Before leaving, his mother asked him where he was going. It was too early, and the school was closed.

"I am going to the park to clear my head. I need to focus," he responded.

"Okay, but be careful. Good luck!" yelled his mother.

When he arrived at the park, there were several people jogging. He sat down on one of the benches and began going over words in his head.

He decided to go to school an hour later. When Tom got there some of his friends were outside.

"Where have you been? I have been looking for you. Are you nervous?" asked Ricky, a friend of his since first grade.

"I went to the park. I needed to concentrate. I was nervous, but I'm feeling better now," he stated.

When Tom and his friends walked into the auditorium, it was packed with students as well as adults. Tom quickly went on stage to join the other competitors. Twenty students were competing. There was much commotion in the auditorium. People were talking and taking pictures. Although the competitors were talking and acting calm and collected, the growing tension on stage was evident.

After a few minutes, a bell rang. It was a signal to let everyone know that they needed to take their seats. The contest was about to start.

One by one, the competitors walked to the front of the stage in an attempt to spell the given words correctly. After two hours, two members remained. Tom was one of them.

A young girl stood in the front of the stage and waited for the given word.

"The word is feuilleton. The word is a noun, which means a part of a newspaper or magazine devoted to fiction, criticism, or light literature. Once again, the word is feuilleton. Good luck," the pronouncer stated.

The girl closed her eyes and paused for a moment. "I am ready. F-e-u-i-l-e-t-o-n."

"I am so sorry. The spelling is wrong."

The girl lowered her head in disappointment and returned to her seat. It was Tom turn.

"Once again, the word is feuilleton. Do you want the definition and other relevant information?"

"No. That's okay," Tom said.

"I am ready. F-e-u-i-l-l-e-t-o-n."

The pronouncer looked up at Tom and smiled. "Congratulations, you are the winner of the spelling contest."

The people in the audience began applauding loudly.

Tom stood in front of the stage with his mouth and eyes wide opened as if in disbelief. He could not believe he had just won the contest. His mother, who was in the audience, had tears in her eyes.

For days, Tom was enjoying his newly acquired fame. It was the onset of Tom's grandiose sense of self-importance. The ego had taken charge. Although he continued to hang out with his childhood friends, he saw himself as superior and treated them as his sidekicks. His father's words kept ringing in his ears: "The strong survive and the weak perish."

Tom entered high school the following year. He continued to excel in academics as well as sports. His ego was much inflated. He began associating with a new group of friends. The group was known to ridicule the weak and helpless. They were ruthless and uncaring. Tom had become the ringleader of the group. By now, the thought of, "the strong survive and the weak perish" was strongly cemented in his mind.

One day, a new student arrived at the school. He was assigned to Tom's class. He stood in front of the class while the teacher introduced him.

"Class, this is Farid. He is a new student who will be a part of this class. Welcome, Farid. Take a seat in the second row."

Farid was a skinny young boy of average height with olive skin and jet-black hair. He was dressed in modest clothing and worn-out sneakers.

His family had escaped from Iran due to religious persecution. He was the eldest of three children. The parents and children were staying with a close relative who had lived in the States for more than twenty years and had become a citizen.

Farid's parents believed that education was the key to a better life and encouraged their children to excel. While living in Iran, Farid was an exceptional student who maintained an A average in all subjects. His father would always tell his children, "Study hard and get a good education. People can take away all your material goods but they can't take away your academic accomplishments."

Although Farid demonstrated that he was extremely intelligent, he was having a difficult time mastering the English language. He read and understood the language, but could not speak it properly.

Tom was like a tiger waiting to ambush and go for the kill. Farid was the perfect prey for his sadistic gratification. Soon, he began teasing and mocking Farid. A day did not go by without Tom and his friends bullying Farid. The everyday stress caused Farid's grades to drop drastically.

"Hey, camel riding dumb-ass. Why are you still here? Take your stinking ass back to the hellhole you came from. We don't want your kind here," Tom shouted, as Farid was opening his locker to get his books.

Everyone who heard the statement started laughing. Farid endured the harsh insults silently. He lowered his head and with tears in his eyes walked away. The harassment continued, some days stronger than others. Farid never defended himself against his attackers. He did not know how. He felt hopeless and alone.

One day, the class was chatting and fooling around. The homeroom teacher had not arrived. Farid was also missing. A few minutes later, the teacher walked in and directed the students to take their seats.

"It saddened me to tell you that one of our students will no longer be among us. Farid died last night. He committed suicide. The school counselor will be visiting the classroom to assist with any feelings you may have pertaining to this matter," the teacher said.

The students looked at each other in disbelief. Some had tears in their eyes.

Tom, who appeared indifferent, looked at his friend who was sitting next to him and whispered, "He took my advice and went to hell." His friend chuckled.

That evening, Tom related the news to his parents. Although his mother expressed some concern, his father did not.

"The world will be a better place without their kind. He would have grown up, moved back to Iran and become a terrorist. That's what they do. God is cleaning the Earth of all the garbage. Remember what I told you. The strong survive and the weak will perish," the father said proudly.

Tom graduated from high school with honors. He was accepted to a prestigious college. In college, he kept outshining in all levels. He continued to associate with his selected group of friends and continued to look down on those he considered his inferior.

After finishing his undergrad studies, Tom decided to continue his education. After two years, he graduated with an MBA. It was the proudest moment in his parents' lives.

Two years later, Tom's father died of a massive heart attack leaving his mother alone in an empty house. One of his brothers had died a few years earlier, while the other had moved far away contacting his mother once a year. Tom was the only son who lived nearby.

A few years later, Tom convinced his mother to sell the house and move into an assisted living apartment. Although she did not want to, Tom was very persuasive and unrelenting.

"The situation will be much better for you. You will have someone available to assist you 24 hours. I am too busy and can't be around to help you," Tom said.

"I understand, but I don't need to go anywhere. I can still take care of myself and this house," she replied.

"No, the decision has been made. It is the best choice for you. You will see that I am right," Tom responded.

During her stay in assisted living, Tom's visits were rare. When she fractured her hip, she was placed in a home. His visits were even more sporadic, calling the home once a month to ascertain how his mother was doing. He had shut her out of his life, forgetting the generosity and many sacrifices she made in order for him to accomplish his dreams.

Tom had no problem acquiring a job. His credentials helped him to secure a good paying job with numerous opportunities for advancement in the banking industry. He rapidly became a rising star procuring several promotions in a short period.

He met Lisa soon after attaining his first promotion. She was an executive secretary, who worked in another department. Besides her physical beauty, she was extremely intelligent. They started dating and, after two years, got married. Lisa insisted on going to India on their honeymoon. She had always dreamed of visiting India. Tom, who was reluctant at first, finally acquiesced.

While in India, Tom insisted on staying in the best luxury hotel in Mumbai. The first time he encountered poverty on the streets of Mumbai, he was appalled. Lisa had insisted on going shopping. They took a cab and headed to the shopping district. As they walked around, they were approached by a homeless little boy and sickly elderly man. The boy and man were not only filthy, but they possessed a foul-smelling odor. Their clothes were torn and soiled, and they were shoeless.

"Sir, please give a rupee or two…food. We hungry… not eat all day," the boy said in broken English.

Tom made no attempt to disguise the repugnance he was feeling. "Get away from us, you filthy animal, or I'll call the police," Tom exclaimed in profound rage.

"Please, police no...no, police. Sorry, sir. We very hungry. No police. Sorry, forgive me. I forgive sir. Lord Shiva bless sir," the little boy said, with tears in his eyes and visibly shaken. The little boy grabbed the old man and quickly walked away.

Tom gazed at them with immense disgust. He was irate by their presence.

Lisa, who had witnessed the entire incident, looked at Tom and said with a smirk on her face, "Can we go shopping now?"

"Next time you want to go shopping, you will have to go by yourself. Everything around here is dirty. This entire place should be flushed down the toilet. Why would you want to come here? From now on, I will be staying by the pool," he told Lisa.

Lisa smiled and stated, "Honey, you are too much."

That was the last time they visited India or any similar country. Tom and Lisa's vacations were on cruises where Tom would sip martinis and mingle with people he felt were his equal.

Things were going well. Tom had been promoted to a more prestigious position, purchased a house in an upscale neighborhood, and was the father of two children.

Tom, who was promoted to a managerial position in the auditor department, was settling into his new office. He had called a brief meeting in the conference room. When the staff arrived, Tom, with a stoic demeanor, greeted them as they walked in. Everyone took a seat and waited for Tom to speak.

"As you know, I will be the new manager of this department. In time, I will be making some changes but for now things will remain the same. I expect punctuality and topnotch work. I will not settle for less. I have an open door policy. So, if you need to share any work related issues, feel free to come into my office. Thank you all for coming. Now, let's get back to work."

Marie was Tom's new secretary. She had worked for the company fifteen years. The last three years, she was taking care of her mom, who had had a stroke. Although her mother had a home attendant, she would always assist when she got home from her work by feeding and bathing her mom. Since she was an excellent and reliable worker, her previous boss had granted permission for her to come an hour later. For two years, she came in at eight and left at four. Now, that her boss had been promoted and Tom was the new manager, she hoped things would remain the same.

One day, the home attendant was unable to go to work due to a sudden sickness. The agency called Marie and told her that they were sending another home attendant who would arrive by ten. Marie called the office and said she would be arriving a bit late. When Marie arrived to work, Tom called her into his office.

"I am so sorry, I was late. My mother's home attendant got sick and I had to wait for another one," Marie revealed.

"We have to separate personal problems from our jobs. I cannot tolerate tardiness in any of my subordinates. If you are having problems with your mother's home attendants, you should consider putting her in a nursing home. There, she will have 24 hours assistance. I foresee this as being a potential problem in the future. I need a secretary who is reliable and on time. I am recommending that you be transferred to another department," Tom said unsympathetically.

Although she wanted to say so much, the words would not come out. She felt as if someone had slapped her hard across her face leaving her dazed.

"You will be notified about your transfer by the end of the week. Now, please excuse me. I have work that I need to finish," he said, ending the meeting.

Marie got up quickly and walked out. She went to the bathroom. Struggling to maintain her composure, the tears kept pouring consistently down her face.

"What just happened? How can a person be so cold?" she asked herself.

She remained in the bathroom for a while. When she calmed down, she went to her desk and started working. For two days, she came in, worked and avoided speaking to Tom. By the end of the week, a memo of her transfer arrived. Although she was sad to leave her co-workers, she desperately wanted to detach herself from Tom. She felt she could not work for someone who was so insensitive and heartless.

As always, Tom left work and passed by an elderly homeless man who had found a permanent spot on the corner. Day in and day out, the homeless man would look at Tom and say, "Sir, I am hungry. Can you buy me coffee?"

At first, Tom looked at him with aversion and replied, "Get a job, you pathetic old man!" However, his tactics changed: he ignored him as if he did not exist.

One day, while leaving his job, Tom and a senior executive officer were talking while going to the garage to get their cars. As usual, the old man was in his spot.

"Can you buy me some coffee?" he said.

"Here is some money. Get yourself a good meal, Buddy," the executive officer responded.

The homeless man smiled and blessed the executive numerous times.

Tom was outraged. "Why would you do that? You are feeding the disease!"

The executive officer smiled and said, "Life is about helping each other."

As Tom got into his car, he thought that the executive was such a fool. He recalled his father's words, "The strong will survive and the weak will perish."

Tom was driving home when it began to rain heavily. The visibility was poor. He kept wiping his windshield, but could only see rain, darkness, and the distant lights of oncoming traffic. He reduced his speed and cautiously drove. A minute or two later, he noticed the lights of a vehicle moving towards him from the opposite side of the road. The vehicle was speeding. He tried pulling to the shoulder of the road, but was too late. The truck was already on top of him. When he woke up, he saw that he was outside of his car lying on the ground.

"Oh, my God, what a scare! The impact was so great that it threw me out of my car. I am so lucky to be alive. Look at the size of that truck. My car is completely destroyed. That idiot almost killed me," he said to himself.

As he looked around, he noticed emergency vehicles parked near the two vehicles. Two emergency workers were running with a stretcher. They started pulling a body out of one of the vehicles. Tom heard one of the ambulance workers say that the driver must have had a massive heart attack and lost control of the vehicle.

"This one also didn't make it," the ambulance worker said to a highway officer.

"Were there more people involved in the accident? How could that be? I only see two vehicles. Perhaps, there were two people in the truck," Tom wondered.

As he approached the body in the stretcher, he was aghast with what he saw. He jumped back and remained frozen. It was his body that was on the stretcher. Tom was confused. At first, he could not grasp what was happening but eventually concluded that it was part of a dream.

"How could this be? I am here and there at the same time. I must be having a nightmare. Yes, that's it. I am dreaming," he uttered.

Tom felt relaxed as he roamed the area witnessing the commotion around him. He had convinced himself that he was dreaming. Even the idea that he stayed dry while it rained did not bother him. Anything was feasible while dreaming.

Suddenly, everything turned pitched black. He could not see anything. The rain, highway lights, moving cars, and rotating lights from the emergency vehicles were gone. He began experiencing immense fear.

He yelled, in growing despair, "I need to wake up. Wake up…wake up…wake up."

Nothing occurred. The notion that everything was part of a dream vanished. The experience he was living was too real. He lingered in darkness, fearful and without a clue of what was occurring. Unexpectedly, a cold breeze emerged. Tom could not detect where it was coming from. The breeze quickly turned into a powerful wind. It felt like a spiraling tropical storm wind with immeasurable speed. The propelling force moved him with accelerating speed traveling in a downward spiral. He was completely powerless.

Then, he was no longer moving. He found himself in a dark, unfamiliar place where the air was tainted by a nauseating odor. There was darkness everywhere. He noticed that he was lying in a revolting and fetid swamp. When he tried to get up, he could not. He felt as if a powerful magnet kept him stuck in the water. He was like a fly trapped in a spider's web.

Although it was pitch black all around him, oddly enough, he was able to see clearly his torso and legs. The sight was hideous. The areas were covered with immense bloody sores and rotting flesh. The sores were so deep that the bones were visible. A mixture of blood and a black thick fluid oozed continuously out of the sores. Hundreds of ravenous worms kept crawling in and out of the sores feeding on the rotting flesh. The pain was excruciating. Tears mixed with sweat and blood bathed his face. He felt defenseless and captive by an intangible force. At first, he cursed the driver that caused the accident. However, he realized it was useless since no one heard him. He was all alone and trapped in an infernal abyss.

"This is definitely not a dream. I am no longer in my physical body. I never believed in life after death, spirits, or anything pertaining to that subject matter. However, here I am in a world unlike the one I was accustomed to. This is real. Life continues after death," he said repeatedly, as abundant tears continued gushing down his face.

He was tormented by constant pain-filled memories of the past. The faces of his mother, Farid, Marie, the homeless man near his work place, the little Indian boy and elderly man and others invaded his thoughts. During such recollecting, he could feel deep inside him the painful suffering and humiliation they endured due to his relentless and cruel verbal attacks. The pain emanating from his decaying flesh and past memories was too much for him to sustain.

"Stop! Please, stop this. I can't bear it any longer," he shouted desperately. However, the tortures of the vivid memories and pain continued.

He wept frantically as a lost child in a vast labyrinth unable to find his way back home. His feelings of apprehension continued to intensify. He wanted to escape, but could not. There was no way out.

Then, he heard a wailing sound. Although it was near, he could not distinguish where it was coming from. The darkness prevented him from seeing anything expect his own body.

His heart commenced to beat faster. He felt excited knowing that someone was near.

"I can't believe someone is close by. Hello, can you hear me?" He shouted. No one replied. Just a moaning sound was heard.

The incessant groaning kept growing louder and louder. Then, it stopped. A fuming voice was now heard. It was shouting blasphemies at God.

"God, I blame you for my present state. However, I will not remain here for long. I know Satan will rescue me, for I have served him well all my life. I hate and curse you. Satan is my only god. He is the true god," the voice shouted while releasing a sinister laugh.

Once again, another voice spoke. It was coming from the opposite direction. This time, the sound was different. It was a sound as if someone were in severe anguish.

"Dear God, please forgive me. I was foolish and wasted my entire life hating and blaming others for my physical disabilities. I even hated and blamed you for all my mishaps. I was so full of hate that I could not see your divine light. Now, I know it is time to pay for all my cruel earthly actions. Forgive me, and may your will be done. Have mercy on my soul," the voice said, with an inconsolable weeping sound heard periodically.

Tom's desperation and fear continued to intensify. He could hear the voices, but could not link with anyone. "Hello, can anyone hear me? I need help," he shouted several times. Again, no response was received.

A while later, a face began to emerge from the darkness. Tom blinked his eyes several times as if skeptical. "Is someone really coming to rescue me?" he thought to himself. As the image continued to manifest itself, Tom became elated.

"Finally, someone I can speak to!" Tom whispered.

When the image ultimately revealed itself, it was a heinous, frightening, grotesque-looking face with piercing angry eyes staring at him.

"Who are you?" Tom said in a terrified tone.

"I am you," the image said with a sinister sounding voice.

"No, that cannot be. You are not me!"

The image's baleful glare petrified Tom.

After a brief pause, the image spoke again. "But, I am. I am a product of your creation. I reside inside you."

"No, you are not me. Get away from me," Tom shouted hysterically.

After unleashing an ear-piercing laughter, the image continued.

"I began to surface the very instant you began feeling superior to others. Your insatiable lust for attention, power, superiority and wickedness gave me what I needed to flourish. Every destructive seed you planted along your terrestrial path created the monster you see in front of you. Your actions made me more resilient and superior. In time, we became one.

"Remember the time mother begged us not to sell her home and move her to an assisting living apartment? We disregarded her feelings and shipped her away. When she was placed in a nursing home and craved some attention and love, we abandoned her. That was great. We didn't need her anymore. And, Farid, who took his life because he couldn't deal with our abusive behavior towards him. That was our most monumental work of art. He was such a weakling. Marie was a good one. We definitely went for the kill. She never had a chance. And, let's not forget the Indian boy, the elderly man, the homeless man, as well as countless others who claimed to have suffered because of us. What nonsense! We were survivors; and they were not. They were all useless and pathetic individuals. As father would say, 'The strong survive and the weak perish.' He was so right."

"Stop it! I don't want to hear anymore. You are not me," Tom said in a rage.

The image laughed and said, "I am you, and you are me. We are one."

The laughter grew stronger as the image faded slowly.

After having the confrontation with the gruesome image, everything remained still. The encounter left him dazed. Then, amidst the darkness, a group of beings dressed in white with a glowing light around them appeared. They remained silent staring at Tom.

"Help me! I don't belong here. I am not a criminal. I am a man of means. I am a highly educated man with several degrees and work for a well-known company. I have never done anything wrong to anyone. I am not a low life. I am a good man. Get me out of here now. Please, help me," Tom exclaimed.

The beings remained quiet as he babbled on frenetically. Without any warning, the individuals of light vanished, leaving Tom, once again, alone in the darkness.

"Please, don't go. Don't leave me here. Come back. I don't belong here." Tom cried out.

Angry and distressed, Tom tried once again to free himself from the water that was keeping him captive. He was like a madman trying to escape the demons of his mind. As he tried pulling himself free, he could feel his flesh ripping from his body causing immense pain and suffering.

Although the skin was tearing off, the body remained bonded to the bottom of the water. There was no way out.

As time passed, Tom began reviewing his life on Earth. The words of his father began ringing in his ears: "The strong survive and the weak perish."

"He was so wrong. I had always been strong, and look at me now. I thought I was on top of the world. But, in reality I was at the bottom. My house, cars, job, etc. didn't matter. In a blink of an eye, I lost everything. I thought I was better than others; I was completely mistaken. I treated people badly, not caring about anything. Now, no one cares about me. I am here alone, abandoned by all. I deserted God a long time ago, and now He has forsaken me. Forgive me, Father," Tom reflected.

Not once, during his earthy existence, did he care about the feelings of others. Now, his past was haunting and forcing him to face his demons. After considering all the details of his life, he was overtaken completely by a sentiment of shame. Tears began pouring out of him continuously.

Tom continued to pray to God asking for His help and forgiveness. This was the first time he bowed down to anyone and admitted his arrogance and culpability. There was a sense of humility in his words.

The beings of light appeared after what seemed to be like an eternity. One of them grabbed Tom and pulled him out of the water. Tom was extremely weak and could not walk. They lifted and carried him into the light. Tom had lost consciousness.

Tom was removed from the world of darkness and transported to a realm of light. He was taken to a spiritual hospital where he remained in a spiritual coma for some time. When he woke up, he was surprised to see the individual that was assisting him. It was Farid. He was dressed in white and covered in a white luminous light. His eyes were full of compassion and love. Farid gently stroked his head and said, "Don't worry. You are safe here. Everything is going to be okay." Once again, Tom went into a deep sleep.

The warmth and brightness of sunrays had just entered the room when Tom opened his eyes. He took a deep breath and turned his head to see Farid seating by his side.

"How are you feeling?" Farid asked.

"I feel much better. But, how come you are here? Where am I?" Tom responded.

"In time all will be made known to you. Right now, it is important for you to rest and recover. I will be back later." Farid said his farewells and walked out.

Tom stood up and began looking around the room. It was immaculate with simple furnishings. The room contained a bed, a night table, and a chair. As he lay back and closed his eyes, he quickly saw an image of his sores. Instantly, he sat up, opened his shirt and examined his torso. The sores were gone. Even his legs were cleaned. He rubbed his chest and legs as if looking for some sign of opening or cut. There was none. His spiritual body was clean of all sores. He got up from bed and walked around. He was surprised that he was feeling strong and pain-free. It was as if every discomfort was magically removed from him.

"Oh, so you are up. Are you ready to take a walk?" Farid asked as he walked in.

"Yes!" Tom said anxiously.

They entered a garden filled with flowers of all sorts that emitted a sweet and calming fragrance. There were blossoming trees that beautified the area. A gentle, caressing breeze scented the air with a pleasant aroma. The sky was an indescribable radiant blue color that added more beauty to the panorama. The far-away chirping sound of birds was like music to the ears. Fascinated by the stunning beauty all around him, he could not stop thinking of God's greatness. The entire scene could only be created by God. It was a true work of art.

They sat down in one of the many benches. Other individuals had gathered in the garden. They were talking, reading and admiring the beauty around them.

"Where am I?" Tom inquired.

"You are in a realm far away from Earth and the realm of darkness in which you were recently a prisoner. This is one of the realms of light.

Here we take care of newly arrived souls who are in need of healing. The building you see in front of you is a healing center. Some refer to it as a 'spiritual hospital.' Spirit rescuers brought you here from a lower realm where darkness and suffering prevails."

"I had given up all hope of being saved. I thank God for allowing His spirit rescuers to come and take me out of that dark and dreadful place. The suffering I endured was horrific.

"And, you? What are you doing here? But first forgive me for all the torments I put you through," Tom expressed.

"I forgave you a long time ago. In order to understand why I am here I must commence at the very beginning. Only then will you understand the bond we share," Farid said.

"During one of my earthly journeys, I lived in Iran. My family and I were subjected to the most horrendous treatment. Due to our religious beliefs, we were persecuted. My uncle, while walking home from work, was shot in the back causing permanent spinal cord damage. A few months later, he died of complications. No arrest was made. One day, my grandfather went to the market and never came back. He was arrested and killed. We were never told why he was arrested. We lived in constant fear of my father having the same fate as my grandfather and uncle. Shortly after the demise of my grandfather, my father decided to move the family to the United States. When we arrived in America, I thought things would be much different. However, it was not.

"Fear was my steady companion. It remained by my side day and night. It intensified when I was assigned to your class. Every morning fear was there to greet me. I tried very hard to let go of the fear, but it would not leave. I prayed to Allah every day. I pleaded that you and your friends would vanish from the face of the earth, but to no avail. Each day, you and your friends were more than ready to torment me. One day, I decided to take matters into my own hands. I was overwhelmed with all that was happening around me. I couldn't face another day of being persecuted. I wanted to escape or run away. My only option was to end my suffering by committing suicide. I pretended to be sick and waited for everyone to leave the house. I grabbed a telephone cord, stood on a chair, firmly tied one end of the cord around my neck, attached the other end to a ceiling fan and kicked the chair away. Since I was very thin, my weight did not affect the stability of the fan. It took a few minutes before my body shut down. It was an agonizing horrible death.

"I always read and believed that when a person died, he or she would go to heaven and live in paradise. All emotional anguish and pain would be left behind. You would get a clean slate and live happily ever after. However, the fact of the matter was another reality. Instead of entering a heavenly realm, I ended in an abyss of darkness.

"When my soul detached itself from my physical body, I remained nearby. There were no white light, tunnel or relatives waiting to greet me. It was just me standing in front of my lifeless body.

"Suddenly, the door opened. It was my mother. 'Farid, I have a surprise for you. I purchased your favorite...' There was silence, and then a scream. A minute or two later, she was unconscious on the floor.

"She had returned from food shopping with my sister. She was quite cheerful when she opened the door to my room. She wanted to surprise me with my favorite ice cream and cookies.

"Seeing the expression on her face was a thousand times worse than all the suffering I endured in school. Her initial reaction and loss of consciousness were heartbreaking to witness.

'Madar, please get up, forgive me!' I shouted.

"She remained motionless. All the shouting was useless. No one could hear me.

"She was rushed to the hospital. Although I wanted to accompany her, I could not. A profound force kept me in the room to view repeatedly the suicide act and the dreadful impact it created. I became the spectator of my grisly act of cowardice. The experience was unbearable. I screamed several times, 'I want to go back into my body. I don't want to be dead.' However, they were words that went nowhere.

"After several times of reliving my suicide and mother's reaction, I found myself being thrust into a dark hole with great intensity. Faster and faster, I moved until I suddenly stopped. I ended up in a dark and gloomy place. A strong nauseating stench was in the air. I had a difficult time breathing. When I looked around, I saw countless zombie-like souls with gruesome faces and lifeless eyes walking aimlessly. In addition, there were animalistic looking creatures with long, sharp fangs attacking and tormenting the condemned souls. Constant screams for help were heard.

"In my attempt to free myself from the terrestrial suffering, I committed the morbid act of suicide and ended up in an inferno.

'Hello, can you help me?' I asked.

"The souls would stop, stare at me, and continue walking. No verbal exchange was made. Some of the souls had bullet wounds in their heads with blood gushing out; several had deep cuts on their wrists with blood dripping; others had purplish marks around the necks with ashen complexion and protruding eyes; and others had scorched bodies. Undoubtedly, this dark place was the home of suicide victims.

"I yearned for the warmth of my family. I felt like a prisoner in a dungeon cell. I ran and ran trying to escape that ghastly place but only to end at the same starting point. Time passed, and my loneliness and desperation grew to infinite heights.

"I was terrified. I supplicated for someone to help me flee from that place. But, to no avail.

"I cried and prayed. I was constantly tortured by visions of my mother's grieving face, her screams and her motionless body. I despised and blamed you and your friends for being the culprits of all the misery in my life. I was full of immense animosity and bitterness. I wanted you and your friends to suffer and cursed you ceaselessly.

"As I continued experiencing mental anguish and pain, a beam of light appeared. It was similar to a shining star. It just stood in front of me for a short while and disappeared. After an incalculable time in darkness, the beam of light appeared again only to disappear quickly.

'Could this be the mind playing tricks on me? Was this another form of God tormenting me?' I questioned myself.

"Time passed without any changes. I remained in darkness constantly reliving the vision of my mother's anguish face and dreadful suicide act. The zombie-like creatures continued to move around aimlessly making ear-splitting noises while vile animalistic creatures roamed the area attacking whoever was near.

'Will I become like them soon?' I wondered. The thought frightened me. I continued to pray.

"After a long time, the beam of light, once again, appeared. This time, it transformed into a recognizable being. It was an elderly man wearing a white tunic. His hair was white and long. He came towards me and spoke.

'I have been sent from above to assist you. You will not be able to leave this place at this time. Although there is much sincerity in your soul, the soul remains contaminated with ill emotions of hate. You need to truly recognize that you generated your present suffering. You committed the greatest sin. You destroyed, by your own hand, the gift of life, which was given to you by God. Remember, Thou shall not kill.'

'Please, forgive me. I was overwhelmed with all the problems I was confronting at the time. I regret all,' I said, as the tears kept streaming out of me.

'Reflect on your actions and continue praying,' the being said.

'How long will I be punished for my transgressions?' I asked in despair.

'Time is measured by your actions and the status of your soul. For some it can be an eternity.' The being began fading away slowly.

'Please, don't go. Don't leave me here. Please, help me. I need to know what happened to my mother,' I said. However, it was too late. The being had gone and darkness reappeared.

"I continued to be tortured by the scene of my actions and my grieving mother. I prayed for forgiveness. I even began praying for you.

"After an incalculable amount of time, the elderly man appeared again. This time, he held his hand out and grabbed mine. With tears of emotion, I took a deep breath. I was finally leaving that hellish place. I was so weak that I couldn't move without his assistance. As we moved upward, the darkness began to dissipate slowly. When we got to the other side, everything was bright. I kept my eyes closed. I had been in darkness so long that my eyes needed to adjust to the change. My elderly friend bought me here. This is where my healing commenced. I worked hard to cleanse my soul and understand the various stages of soul development. My elderly friend saved me and helped me along the way.

"It took a long time before I was able to visit my earthly mother.

She always sensed my presence. She had become an invalid after having a stroke. She lived to be a very old person who accepted her fate with much love and resignation. Recently, she made her transition to the spirit world and returned home. God is merciful.

"After a long period of regeneration and healing, I was given the opportunity to re-enter Earth in flesh form. I decided to live a life of immense poverty in Mumbai, India. During that lifetime, my parents died when I was three years old. I lived with my elderly paternal grandfather. He was a feeble sick man. We lived in a tiny corrugated iron shack in the slum area in Mumbai. There was no running water or electricity. Every day, we went out and begged for something to eat. On many occasions, we went to bed without eating. One day, we met you. I was a skinny undernourished seven years old. Do you remember? You were irate and disgusted by our presence. After cursing and insulting us, I said to you, 'Sorry, forgive me. I forgive sir. Lord Shiva bless sir.' A few weeks later, my grandfather's heart gave up. He died in his sleep. And, a year later, while crossing the busy streets of Mumbai, I was hit by a car and died. I came to Earth on a mission and fulfilled it.

"God gave me the opportunity to come to Earth to confront you, ask for forgiveness and forgive you. I was able to eradicate the hatred emanating from the previous lifetime where I took my life.

"Then, when I heard that you were coming to this realm, I volunteered to assist you in your healing process. That is the reason I am here.

"I blamed you and your friends for my mother's condition and my imprisonment in the realm of darkness. I hated you and your friends and wanted retribution. The longer I held on to these emotions, the deeper I submerged in a sea of darkness. It was my elderly friend who made me realize how crucial it was to let go of negative earthly emotions and begin the process of facing my inner demons. Revenge and hate were not the answer. They were the destruction of my soul. It took me a very long time to come to terms that you were not the cause of my downfall. It was my inner demons, and weakness or fear to confront them. I was placing culpability on the wrong individuals. I was the main source that triggered my mother's illness and my spiritual confinement and suffering. I took my life and went against God's law: 'Thou shall not kill.' This includes self."

Tom was moved to tears after hearing Farid's story. The painful truth of his cruel actions and Farid's story forced him to re-examine his inner self in a profound way. He was able to see the ugliness he possessed inside. He came to the realization that the image he saw while trapped in the realm of darkness was he.

"Farid, once again, please forgive me. I considered you once to be a weak person. Instead, you have proven to be the stronger of the two. I am ashamed of what I once was and did. My soul was hollow. It had no love or compassion for anyone. I was self-absorbed. Even my wife and children suffered because of my demeanor. It was all about me. Your story has made me see how blinded I was," he said in a sorrow-filled voice.

Farid smiled and said, "We all make mistakes. It is up to us to sincerely recognize and rectify our transgressions. It is the beginning of the healing process. However, many souls refuse to acknowledge and let go of their negative feelings or wrongdoings, keeping themselves enslaved in a world of darkness for eternity. We must pray for our brothers and sisters so that they too can admit the errors of their ways and enter the light."

Farid became Tom's mentor, helping him in all stages of his healing and rehabilitation.

After a rather lengthy period, Tom was granted the opportunity to reincarnate. The earthly reincarnation preparations were being made. He was eager to embark on a journey of redemption. This time, he would try to do things differently. It was agreed upon that he would enter a world of immense poverty with insurmountable life challenges. Each member of his new Earth family would be someone from a past life. The souls agreed to reincarnate in the same family in order to put closure. Marie would become his wife; his mother would be his handicapped younger sister; and the homeless man his ailing father.

When he entered the Earth plane, he was welcomed into the world by his mother and ailing father. A few years later, his sister was born. Due to a childhood illness, she was paralyzed from the waist down. At age twelve, his mother passed away. He became the sole provider of the family. His father, who was sickly, suffered from a head injury sustained several years ago. It affected his thought processes and body movements. At age seventeen, Tom married. The couple never had children. The family lived in a one-room shack without running water or electricity. They always had very little to eat, but always shared whatever was available. He treated each member of his family with much love, respect, and compassion. Every morning, he went out to do what was necessary in order to support his family. Although life was extremely arduous, he never gave up and did his best to serve, love, and please his family. He lived to be a very old man. His father, sister, and wife had all passed away before him.

Upon leaving the body, his spirit was greeted by Farid and many other souls. They entered a luminous tunnel and commenced their journey back home.

Although many incarnate souls enter the Earth plane and deviate from their agreed mission, others accomplished their task effectively. Tom was one of the latter. He completed his task fully. He rid himself of past life impurities and debts. He was no longer a prisoner of the past.

Undoubtedly, what goes around comes around. Treat others with respect and kindness. Remember, we are all brothers and sisters connected to God.

CHAPTER 9

THE JOURNEY

It is midday and the sun is burning hot. I have been walking on this isolated road for what appears to me to be an eternity. There are no posts that indicate where I am at or where I am heading. The area is mainly barren with a dried up shrub or two along the side of the road. There is not one tree where I can find shelter from the blazing sun. The sun is merciless. Not even a gentle breeze is blowing. I have blisters on my face, body, and feet. My feet ache and are on fire. When I remove my shoes, my feet are red and swollen. Although I would love to keep my shoes off, I cannot. They protect me from causing further damage to my feet. There are several small jagged stones on the ground. Each step I take is excruciating. However, I must continue walking. I need to find a way out of here.

My lips are parched. My body craves water, but there is none. Although I try to think positive thoughts, my mind knows better and cannot continue the farce. I have walked for hours and not one single person has appeared. Not even the sound of a bird is heard. This loneliness is driving me insane. I don't know how much I can take. I need to rest, but the question is where. I am on a road that is going nowhere.

"What am I doing on the ground?" I say to myself in a state of confusion.

It seems I have passed out. I remember walking slowly and feeling immense heaviness all over my body. Then, everything went blank.

Why did I wake up? I would have preferred to remain unconscious rather than continue on this agonizing journey. I want to die. I don't want to continue wandering through empty valleys and hills.

Desperation has taken over. It continues to heighten without any sign of relief. I cannot contain the tears that are continuously rolling down my face.

"God, help me. Please, have mercy on me," I yell in an agonizing tone.

There is complete silence. It's as if the words evaporated before reaching the Source. There is no doubt in my mind that God has abandoned me.

The day seems eternal. The sun continues to pound relentlessly upon my body. The night has not come, and it seems it will not. I have been walking aimlessly for hours. I am exhausted. I don't know how much more I can endure.

"God, why have you abandoned me? I am wandering on this lonely road without hope of finding my destination, or a helping hand that could bring comfort to my aching heart. What have I done to deserve this? When will this journey end? How much longer will I endure this agony?" I, once again, cry out desperately to the heavens. Still, I receive no answer. I continue to pray although my faith is slowly fading away.

I resume walking endlessly. I stop to rest and look around. I cannot believe I am back where I started. I have gone full circle ending at the same starting point. I feel so defeated and hurt.

"Why is this happening to me?"

Tears have clouded my eyes. Wiping my tears away, I see something not far from me. The image looks blurry from where I am standing.

"Is that a person or a mirage? Am I hallucinating?"

I cautiously get closer. The image becomes better defined. It's an elderly man with long white hair sitting on the side of the road in a yogi position. He is dressed in a long, white robe. His eyes are closed, and he appears to be meditating.

It seems that God has answered my prayers. I am elated. Yes, God has sent this man to help me. There is no other explanation.

The man appears to be in deep thought. I don't want to disturb him, but I need to find out where I am.

"Excuse me, sir, can you help me?" I say politely.

Slowly, he opens his eyes, lifts his head and smiles at me. It's a warm and friendly smile. He signals me to sit and offers me water. I wholeheartedly accept his invitation and offering. The water is so refreshing.

"Where am I?" I ask.

"This road is called the endless road. It leads to nowhere. You can walk forever and eventually find yourself in the same spot where you started," the old man replies.

"Yes, I know. I have been walking for hours without reaching any destination. Is there a way out of here?" I inquire.

"Yes, there is. If you want, I can help you. I'll be happy to show you a road that leads to a place of plenty. It is a place of ample richness, happiness, and merriment. There are numerous people to keep you company and share the experience. You will never feel alone. Come with me and I will show you the way," he states.

Although something inside me is telling me not to go, I ignore the feeling and follow him faithfully.

We go through an opening on the side of the road. It leads to another road. I have passed by this area several times and never noticed this sector. After traveling a short distance through a deserted and uncultivated land, we approach an enclosed area with numerous majestic, towering trees.

We continue walking until we come across a gate. Suddenly, a young man appears. He is the gatekeeper. Upon seeing the elderly man, the gatekeeper rushes over and kisses his hand. The elderly man gently strokes the man's head and commends his good work. The young man smiles and opens the gate.

"You must be very well known here," I mention.

"I have been coming here from the beginning. I consider this place like my home. I bring people here who are lost, tired, and in need of a place to rest."

We walk in and I am enthralled by the beauty and immensity of the place. I remain motionless with my eyes and mouth slightly opened for a few minutes.

"Are you alright?" the elderly man asks.

"Yes, it just that I never expect something like this. In fact, I have never seen a place like this before. This is beautiful."

The elderly man smiles and we continue to walk.

The place is alive with the sound of laughter and chatting. People dressed in fine garments stroll down the streets with smiling faces. They appear to be carefree. Everywhere we go, people stop to greet the elderly man. They bow their heads as an act of great reverence and admiration. The elderly man stops and pats their heads.

"You are truly loved here," I interject. He smiles and remains silent.

"This place is quite stunning. Thank you for bringing me here." Once again, the elderly man smiles and continues walking.

The area is full of artistic richness and splendor. The streets are paved with gold while superb looking buildings and private homes embellish the area. All of the structures are painted white with touches of marble and precious stones carvings adorning the facades. Colorful flowers and magnificent trees add to the exquisiteness of the scenery. The relaxing sound of chirping birds is heard in the background. There is a sense of gaiety in the air.

The sun is shining and there is not one cloud across the sky. The sun is no longer pounding on me. Instead, it is bathing me with its warm light. A gentle breeze caresses my face. I no longer feel alone or desperate. I feel I have finally reached my true destination.

The elderly man calls a young woman over. He introduces me. Her name is Maria.

"Maria, I want you to show her around," he says before leaving.

"Don't worry. I will take care of her. Farewell," she replies.

"Go with her. She will be your guide. Enjoy yourself," he utters.

"I will. Thank you so much," I reply. Before leaving, I bow my head and kiss his hand.

Maria is a twenty-five-year-old woman with a slender build and medium height. She has a golden complexion and a lovely smile. She is extremely friendly with a jovial sense of humor.

"Come, let me show you around. You are going to love this place," she says.

We enter a building with massive doors. The entrance hall is of vast proportions with impressive large columns all around. The area is richly decorated with an assortment of eclectic artwork from famous artists throughout history. In the center of the hall is an enormous staircase leading to the second floor. The stair banisters are made of gold and precious stones. A substantial size crystal chandelier hangs in the center of the ceiling. It is magnificent.

As I walk up the stairs, I cannot help admiring the craftsmanship of the banisters and the sparkling variety of magical colors shooting out from the crystal chandelier.

People begin to greet us as we enter one of numerous rooms on the second floor. The décor of the room consists of lush drapes, silk rugs, fine leather sofas and much more. Golden sunlight floods in through three oversize windows giving immense brightness and warmth to everything around. An enormous table filled with a variety of delicacies and fine wines is set up for the enjoyment of all.

As I move around the room, I see people laughing, conversing, smoking, and consuming food and beverages. They all seem to be quite friendly and happy.

"Here, drink some of this," Maria says while handing me a glass.

"I don't drink alcohol."

"This isn't alcohol. This is similar to a health drink but much better.

It clears your senses and lifts your spirit."

"Okay, I'll try some," I respond.

The drink actually has a great taste and is very addictive. After a few drinks, I am feeling euphoric and free of all inhibitions. I become part of the group. Everyone is making me feel at home. I no longer think of the past or the endless journey I was on. I don't know how or when but I begin smoking. I have never smoked before, but now I am enjoying it fully. The combination of the smoke and beverage provides a means in which I can step out of my present reality and visit other dimensions. My head begins to spin but it's a wonderful sensation. Beautiful colorful nebulas appear dancing around in my head. I see myself flying in the vastness of the universe. Unimaginable colors appear before my eyes.

We continue to party for several days or weeks. I don't know exactly because time here is inconsequential. To my amazement, I am neither sleepy nor tired. After a while, the rapturous experience wears off. I look for Maria, but she is nowhere to be found. I leave in an attempt to seek more pleasure.

I go from door to door of the various rooms on the second floor, but they are all locked. I head down the stairs and out the door. I enter various houses along the way and engage in similar activities as before. However, my body is never satisfied and craves for more. It's as though I have become addicted to the numerous pleasures offered in this domain.

I roam around the area in pursuit of more profound gratifications. I feel like a junkie looking for his next fix. Suddenly, I stop and sense a noticeable feeling in the air. The air feels denser and polluted. As I continue to walk, the sun begins to hide behind a dark cloud.

"Where did that cloud come from?" I ask myself.

The further I walk, the darker it gets. The sun is no longer visible.

"Where am I? What is this place?" I wonder.

The streets are not paved with gold. Instead, they are covered with dirt, grime, and red-colored stains. The air carries an odor of stench, which is overpowering. The sound of chirping birds has been replaced by a gruesome moaning sound. I keep on moving with much trepidation. Although I feel someone staring at me, I look all around but see no one. Beads of sweat begin to appear on my forehead. It is not a comfortable situation. I turn around to go back, but the darkness has obscured the passage.

Suddenly, a little old lady appears sitting on the ground near a lamp post. She is barefoot and shivering. Her clothes are filthy and ripped. She seems to be crying. When I approach her, a terrible stench emanates from her. I cover my nose. She lifts her head and looks at me. Her face is wet with tears, and her eyes have an empty lifeless look to them.

"Can I help you?" I ask.

"I have been abandoned by my loved ones. I don't have anyone. I have not eaten in days. I don't even know where I am. Please, help me," she says while weeping.

Abruptly, I am hit hard on the back of my head with a blunt object while grabbing her arm to lift her up. I fall to the ground. I feel someone kicking me hard all over my body while others are laughing. I can't see their faces. The beating is too great that I lose consciousness. When I wake up, the little old lady is gone. So is my ring that was a gift from my mother.

"What was that all about? Where is the old lady? Was she part of the scheme to rob me or was she an innocent victim used as a distraction by a malicious criminal gang to trap their future prey?"

I struggle to get up. My entire body hurts, and my head is spinning. There is a sharp pain in the back of my head. I reach over to touch the area; I feel a warm sensation of blood pouring out of my head. I have a deep gash. There is blood everywhere.

"Oh my God, I need to get out of here," I say to myself.

Trembling and panting, I resume moving. My legs are wobbly; my head is throbbing. My body seems to be on fire. Sweat is beginning to pour down my face and body. I desperately need help. With a profound weakness all over my body and stumbling, here and there, I continue to move forward.

I see an old decrepit building not too far from me. "Perhaps, there is someone there that can help me," I pray and hope for it to be true.

The building is an old abandoned church. A man dressed in religious garb is standing in the front. He is reading out loud scriptures from a bible. I am confident that he will assist me.

"Sir, can you help me? I am a catholic and a believer of God. I need help. I was just attacked. I am not feeling well. Please, help me," I say as the sweat and tears continue to bathe my face and body.

The man lifts his head, stares at me with immense anger and begins shouting as if insane.

"Get the fuck away from me you low life earthly scum. If you don't, I will rip your heart out. I said get away from me or I will slice you up and sacrifice you to the Gods. Yes, kill, kill, kill!"

His face has turned red with rage. With his eyes wide open and a tight fist, he spits at me. "I will kill you!" he shouts at the top of his lungs.

I leap back fearing for my life. I walk away quickly. From afar, I hear him read a scripture from the bible, "This is my commandment, that you love one another just as I have loved you."

"What a hypocritical asshole. He doesn't even know the meaning of love," I whisper to myself.

The bleeding has miraculously stopped, but I remain dizzy. I continue staggering. The moaning sound has gotten louder. It's very unnerving. I continue walking until I find myself in front of a cemetery. The place is gloomy and eerie. As I get closer, a cold chill runs down my spine. Instead of tombstones, there are crosses with life-size graphic wax figures nailed to them upside down.

"Oh my God, this is getting very weird."

I take a closer look, and I am horrified at what I see. They are images of saints and holy individuals from all religions known to man. Although their faces have been somewhat distorted, they are still recognizable.

I see a tree nearby. From where I am standing, I see shadowy figures hanging from its branches. I move closer and see the most horrendous scene. The figures are of animals, mostly dogs and cats, who have been skinned and fastened to the tree. Hundreds of flies cover the rotting flesh. The smell is nauseating. I cover my nose and walk away. The scene is too hideous for my eyes.

"What sick person would do this?... What does this mean?... What is this place?... How did I get here?" I ask myself these questions, as I slowly move down the street.

There is a young girl walking alone. Several men are following her. I sense something is going to happen to her. I want to help, but I don't know how. I cannot walk any faster.

Oh my God, they just grabbed her from the back and threw her on the ground. Some of the men have her pinned down while others are raping her. People are walking around oblivious to what is occurring in front of them. They don't care. I need to do something. I see two Police Officers standing nearby.

I force myself to walk a bit faster. The pain in my head is excruciating. I need to do something to help the girl.

"Officers, you need to help a girl who is being raped. Please, come with me. I'll show you," I urge.

They ignore me and continue conversing with each other.

"Officers, don't you understand that a girl is being gang raped. You need to do something."

One of them looks at me and says, "Lady, let me see if I understand you correctly. You want me to investigate a gang raping that you say is happening now. I can't risk getting shot or accused of using too much physical force on any of the perps. I have a wife and children who are waiting for me at home. Go home. At the end, everything will work out fine."

Furious, I shout, "What do you mean everything will work out fine? Aren't you cops? Aren't you supposed to protect and serve the people?"

"Lady, keep it down or else I will have to take you to the precinct."

"What exactly is your job?" I ask frantically.

"My job is to tell people like you to go home and mind your own business. Have a good night." They get in their car and drive off without looking back.

This place is amazing. No one seems to care. I walk back to see about the girl. She is gone. I wonder what happened to her. People continue walking aimlessly. They look like zombies.

Further ahead, I see vast destruction. Only rubble remains where buildings and houses once stood. In some areas, the fire still burns, turning the rubble into a cloud of dust.

Not far from where I am standing, I can hear the sounds of gunfire and bombs going off. I breathe deeply as beads of sweat continue to form on my forehead. My heart is beating faster. I am extremely fearful and sense something terrible is going to happen to me.

A young boy of approximately twelve years old with protruding eyes, a skeletal body, and needle marks on his arms approaches me. "Do you want to get high? Come with me. I have the good stuff."

I ignore him and keep on walking. I hear him yell, "Bitch, don't come back here." I turn around. He is pointing a gun at me and talking foolishness. I keep on walking.

"This place is for the mentally insane. I need to find a way out of here," I keep repeating to myself.

I stop to hear a faint sound coming from a pile of garage on the side of the street. It is the sound of a baby crying. I remove the dirty trash and see a starving baby with a distended belly. The baby has been abandoned here. I pick it up and try to seek help.

"Can you help me? I just found a baby who needs help."

The people ignore me as if I were not there. I wrap the baby in dirty old newspaper I find on the streets. It's the only way to keep the baby warm. I find a building that is partially destroyed with the entrance hall intact. I place the baby inside in a secure area and leave to seek out help.

I observe a group of people congregating not far from me. Perhaps, they can help the child and me.

"I am asking for five pieces of gold for this young thing. She will give you pleasure for many years to come. Do I have an offer?" the man shouts.

The crowd, composed of mainly men, is rowdy. They are eager to inspect and purchase the goods. The merchandise consists of young, innocent children. They are being sold like cattle. Their young faces reveal the pain and suffering they have endured. A little girl, who appears to be four or five years old, is crying hysterically. An old, dirty looking man is inserting his finger up her anus while others are laughing. She is bleeding profusely.

"Leave her alone," I yell.

One man is looking at me in a menacing way. He pulls a knife out of his coat pocket.

"Come here and stop us," he shouts.

I turn around and walk away rapidly. My heart is pounding and knees are shaking. Sweat is pouring heavily down my face. I feel as if my head is about to burst.

"I need to go back and help the baby!" I whisper to myself.

As I come near to the building, I see three men. I slowly move near and hear them talking.

"We can get a good price for these. Today is a good day." They gather some bags and leave.

As I walk into the hallway, there is blood everywhere. Not far from where I am standing, I see a malnourished dog. Although the lighting overhead is sparse, I can clearly see the dog's bones, ribs and spine. It has no body fat. The dog is so busy devouring something that it is unaware of my presence. Unexpectedly, the dog turns around and sees me. He begins to bark and growl. It's jagged, blood-stain teeth are noticeable. Although my knees are quivering, I can't move. I feel a cold chill spreading all over my body. My heart feels like it is about to explode. The dog stops growling and goes back to his previous interest. I remain still. I feel the dog will attack me if I move. A minute or two later, the dog picks up a bloody object from the floor and moves in the direction of the entrance door. Before leaving, he stops and glares at me.

"Is that part of an arm he has in his mouth? No, it can't be, "I whisper to myself.

I look around and notice pieces of discarded flesh everywhere. The men who were here earlier had chopped up the baby to remove the organs, leaving the unwanted flesh to be consume by hungry predators.

"Oh, no! This can't be happening. It is too much for me to digest. How can someone kill an innocent, defenseless child cold-heartedly? What has happened to humanity? Oh, my God, take me away from here. I can't endure anymore," I scream in horror.

I begin to hyperventilate. My heart continues to feel as if it is going to burst out of my chest. Tears begin to pour out of me continuously.

Slowly, I walk down the dark and grimy road. I continue to witness horrendous atrocities. I observe young, starving children selling their tiny bodies for a piece of stale bread; people killing each other senselessly; abandoned children dirty and hungry roaming the streets; women beaten mercilessly by their husbands or boyfriends; youngsters with numerous needle marks desperately looking for another fix; abandoned elderly living in cardboard boxes; people riddled with incurable diseases; religious fanatics destroying everything that comes in their path; animals being slaughtered for personal pleasures; and the list goes on. I don't want to be here. This is not a place of happiness and merriment. This is a place of pure darkness and misery.

"Oh, my God, what have I done? I made a terrible mistake. I selected a path that was short and less burdensome without realizing the heavy penalty attached. I allowed myself to be enticed by the trappings of a world with a dark hidden agenda. Is this what people refer to as hell on earth?"

It is true that not everything that shines is gold. The old man was not a messenger from God as I initially thought. He was the devil disguised as a benevolent human being feeding on my weaknesses and imperfections.

The passage from Matthew 4:1-11 comes to my mind:

> "Again, the devil took him to a very high mountain and showed him all the kingdoms of the world and their splendor. 'All this I will give you,' he said, 'if you will bow down and worship me."
>
> Jesus said to him, "Away from me, Satan! For it is written: Worship the Lord your God, and serve him only. Then, the devil left him, and angels came and attended him."

Although Jesus was a great teacher, undoubtedly, I am a poor student. I wanted immediate gratification and never considered the ramifications of my actions. I allowed myself to be pulled in by the negative energy that waits patiently for its prey. Now, I am a prisoner of this Sodom and Gomorrah situation without an escape plan.

Wanting to take the easy route, I ended here. Instead of trusting in God, and knowing He has a purpose for everyone, I decided not to wait and took the shorter path. At first, I was enjoying the many pleasures of this place. However, I soon reached the conclusion that life is full of numerous trappings to keep us away from the light of God.

"God, forgive me. Help me to get out of here and back to where I started," I implore.

I continue to walk trying to find an exit out of this infernal place. However, the more I walk, the darker it gets. It's impossible to continue walking for I cannot see anything. I sit alone in total darkness. I have no sense of time. It seems I have been here forever. I am like a little child who is scared and defenseless. I sense movement around me, but I cannot see who it is. The energy seems sinister. Even though the noise around me is maddening, I pray ceaselessly.

"Will God rescue me from this darkness?" I can only hope for it to be true.

Instantly, a luminous light appears. The light transforms into an angel. He smiles and takes my hand. My heart is pounding and hands are trembling. I am so nervous. I can't believe that I am finally going to be rescued. He guides me out of the darkness and into the light. He takes me back to the place where I was before meeting the old man. As I turn to thank my savior, he is no longer around. He has vanished without saying good-bye.

"God, forgive me for doubting you. I know now that you were always by my side. I was foolish and selfish. Instead of accepting my earthly trials and tribulations, I took the easy way out. I know that we are here to learn and purify our souls, and the only road to you is the one you have set in front of us. Forgive me and give me strength so that I will not deviate from my true spiritual journey."

Now, I walk the secluded road without complaints. I try to enjoy and take in all I see. I no longer feel lonely or question where I am going. I know God is with me at all time, guiding my footsteps. He is the architect of my life creating a master plan for me.

We know what we want; God knows what we need. Trust God to show you the way.

CHAPTER 10

GREED

A homeless man was sleeping on a desolated road. He had just finishing eating several cashew fruits from a nearby tree and decided to take a nap. It was the only meal he had eaten all day. The shade from the tree kept him cool and protected from the brazing sun.

"James," a voice called out.

The homeless man, who was half asleep and with his eyes closed, turned around and responded, "What!"

"James," the voice said again.

"Leave me alone. Can't you see I am sleeping?" he replied with a tone of aggravation.

"James," the voice repeated once again.

The man, who was now extremely vexed, lifted his head from the ground and opened his eyes. The sun was blocking him from seeing the person's face. However, when he looked closely, he noticed the stranger was wearing a long white tunic.

"Listen, go away and let me sleep," he exclaimed in an abrasive pitch.

"James, I want you to do me a favor," the stranger responded calmly.

"Wait a minute. How do you know my name?" James asked.

"I know everything about you."

By now, James was intrigued and suspicious, at the same time.

"Okay, so you feel you know all about me. Very interesting! How can I help you?"

"I need for you to do me a big favor. I will be going away for a while and need someone to be the caretaker of my land," the stranger replied.

"You want me to take care of your land? And, where is this land? " James asked.

"It is not far from here. Come with me and I'll show you."

The stranger had moved to a shaded area, and James was able to clearly see his face. His hair was dark, curly, and shoulder length. His eyes were dark and large with a magnetic look to them. When he spoke, he did so with an intonation of love and calmness. There was something unusual about the stranger that James could not figure out.

"Follow me, James," the strange said.

James paused momentarily to collect his thoughts. He looked at the stranger and wondered if the man was deranged or telling the truth. Sensing that the stranger was not going to cease from his quest, he decided to play along and appease him. He had nothing to lose.

James got up, dusted off the dirt from his worn and torn clothes, and picked up a stick before following the stranger. The stick was for protection.

"That won't be necessary. I will not harm you," the stranger said with a smile on his face.

James felt awkward. "How did he know what I thinking?" he pondered. He threw the stick to the side of the road and continued walking.

They walked for approximately half an hour before reaching their destination.

"We are here," the stranger said.

Fertile fields with rolling green hills were seen for miles. Numerous large fruit trees, rich orchards, and an assortment of exotic flowers adorned the panorama. From a distance, he could see cattle roaming the pastures feeding on bright green grass. The scene was absolutely breathtaking. By this time, James was all ears, listening attentively to the stranger.

"Is this all yours?" James asked with a tone of excitement in his voice.

"Yes, it is. If you decide to stay, there is something you need to know. The workers who tend to the fields and livestock, reside on the property. They are entitled to an equal share of the crops. It will be your job to see that everything runs accordingly. Remember, everyone gets an equal share of the crops."

"I am a bit confused. Why do you want a homeless man like me to manage this entire property? You don't know me. Why not pick one of your workers?" James replied.

"But I do know you. I know you very well. As for the workers, they already have a mission to fulfill," the stranger responded.

As they walked further in, they came across a white painted house with a large porch in front. An immaculately manicured bright emerald green lawn, numerous trees, shrubs and flowers surrounded the house. It was picture perfect.

When they entered the house, James could not believe the enormity of the interior. It had numerous windows in which the sun poured through making the inside area brighter and warmer. Although the house was furnished in a simple manner, the richness of the objects was undeniable. The upstairs contained several rooms. Each room had the same simple and rich style.

"Oh, my God, this can't be happening to me," James said to himself.

As if listening to his thoughts, the stranger said, "But it is. You can stay in the house and feel free to use all that is available. Come, let me show you more." The stranger signaled James to follow him.

They went outside and walked a few yards away from the house until they approached a barn. When they walked inside, James' eyes widened. The inside was nothing like the outside. The outside looked smaller while the inside was three times larger. All breed of animals imaginable were housed there. Several workers were there tending the flock. James smiled as he was introduced to the workers.

Two days later, the stranger said his farewell to everyone. Before leaving, he told James, "Remember, equal share of the crops for everyone." James nodded his head and smiled.

James settled into his new accommodations. He was still amazed how his luck had turned around. Each day, he would run outside to bask in the sun. He would look at the immensity and beauty of the land and ask himself, "Why me?"

In the beginning, James worked side by side with the workers tending the flock and harvesting the crops. He maintained his promise and shared the crops equally with the workers.

Three years went by without any news from the stranger. James was convinced that he would not return. Slowly, he began viewing himself as the sole owner of the property. His attitude towards the workers started shifting. He worked less and demanded more from them. He had gone from caretaker to master. When the time came to share the crops equally, he gave less.

Joseph was a devoted, honest, and obedient worker who had worked the field from the very beginning. He was highly regarded by the stranger. One day, while working the field, James walked up to him and accused him of stealing.

"The amount of the crop you submitted is less than the usually tally. Where is it? You have stolen from me," James shouted so that everyone could hear.

"Sorry, sir but that is all I have. I have not stolen from you," Joseph said meekly.

"You are a liar and a thief. I'll show you who is in charge here," James said as he got closer to Joseph and struck him across the face. He then took a bamboo stick that was nearby and beat him until he was bloody all over. Not once did Joseph put up a fight.

Facing the group of workers who were present, he shouted, "I want all of you to see what happens to those who attempt to steal from me. Let this be a lesson to all of you."

"And as for you, I want you to take your filthy, lying self and your useless family out of my land," he screamed.

"Sir, please forgive me, but I did not steal from you. Please, don't kick us out. I have no place to go. I have little ones and my wife is pregnant. Please, don't send us away from here. I beg you!" Joseph pleaded as tears mixed with blood covered his face.

"I don't care if you have little ones or your wife is pregnant. I want you out now. If I see you here when I get back, I will chop you up into little pieces," James exclaimed as he walked away.

When James was not around, the workers ran to Joseph to assist him. He was still on the ground bleeding. His clothes and the ground were stained with his blood. He had been beaten so viciously that his face and body were badly swollen and discolored. With the help of the workers, Joseph was taken to his home. There, they helped in packing his stuff. He was placed in a hand pulled cart, while his family walked, and taken to a neighboring village.

From that day, the workers toiled in fear. They labored harder and received less. Meanwhile, James savored the fruit of their labor.

As time went on, the number of workers diminished. Some had died while others ran away to escape the exploitation and cruelty by the hand of James. Only a hand full remained.

James continued to live as a king, relishing all that was available to him. Each morning, he would go out to the field enjoying its beauty and the sweet fragrance of the trees and flowers.

Another year had gone by and still no word of the stranger. James had totally dismissed all thoughts of the stranger from his conscious mind. The image of the stranger had become a distant memory.

One day, James was taking his normal tour of the property. The sun was out caressing the fields as usual. It was another wonderful day. Unexpectedly, the sun disappeared and darkness covered the sky. A strong breeze had settled in.

"I guess the rainy season is coming early this year. That's good. We could use some rain. It has been extremely hot," he said to himself.

The sound of loud thunder broke his train of thought. He ran back to the house and sat down on the front porch. While waiting for the rain to come, he noticed a great deal of thunder, but no rain. For hours, he sat and waited for the rain. He loved to hear the sound of raindrops hitting the roof and windows. The sound gave him inner calmness. After hours of waiting for the rain to come, he decided to go inside the house.

The sun hid behind the darkness of the sky for days. Not even a drizzle of rain came. After a month of constant cloudy skies, the sun began emerging. However, with each passing day, the sun became unbearable with soaring temperatures. A severe drought condition had taken over the region, causing major destruction all around. Due to the hot and dry weather, fires began to develop. The land that James loved had become a disaster zone. There were no longer fruit trees, green meadows, or rich orchards. The animals perished as well. Only their skeletons remained. They died from the heat wave and hunger. Even the house that James adored was gone. It caught fire, leaving only debris and ashes. The one or two workers that remained loyal to him disappeared. James was alone. He came with nothing and was leaving the same way.

James walked for days. The road he was on was barren. He craved food and water, but there was none. He slept on the hot ground while the blazing sun beat down on his emaciated body. His clothes were dirty and soiled. He reeked of a foul odor. He had gone from rags to riches to rags. Tired and hungry, he dragged himself forward. He did not know where he was going and did not care. He dropped to the ground and wept deeply because he was unable to continue.

"God, don't abandon me. I can't go on," he said before losing consciousness.

When James opened his eyes, a person was standing in front of him. He blinked a few times to see clearly the image. His eyes were red with a burning sensation. He kept rubbing them. After a few minutes, the figure began to take form. He could not believe his eyes. It was the stranger.

"Is that you?" James asked.

"Yes, it is I."

"When did you get back?"

"I was never gone. I was always by your side."

James, who voice was barely audible, said, "I don't understand. Who are you?"

"I am Jesus."

James slowly got on his knees and with profound wonderment began to weep.

"Lord, I have failed you. Everything is lost," James said with a tone of remorse in his voice.

"My Father gave you the opportunity to make amends of all your past transgressions. Instead, you added to them. You wrongfully took the role of master and abused those who had been faithful to God. You cheated, thrashed, tortured, oppressed, and enslaved your brothers and sisters. Your desire for power and riches blinded you. You permitted your inner greed and selfishness to control your actions. And, in doing so, you fell into the trap of evilness. In God's eyes, all human beings are equal. However, in your eyes, you deemed them as inferior and you superior. Now, you are where you started. Go and sin no more," Jesus revealed.

James lowered his eyes and wept profusely. "Forgive me, Lord. Please, forgive me."

When he lifted his head, Jesus was no longer standing in front of him. He was alone once again. He got up slowly and proceeded to walk forward. He didn't know where he was going but felt an intangible force guiding his footsteps. For hours, he trekked on the secluded barren road. Suddenly, he fell from exhaustion. Assuming it was his last moment on Earth, he looked up to the sky and said, "Forgive me, Father." As he lay on the ground with his eyes closed, he heard a gentle voice say, "James get up." Opening his eyes, he struggled to get back on his feet. When he got up, he moved unsteadily straight ahead.

An hour had passed when James came across a field of fruitful trees. He quickly grabbed one of several mangos that had fallen from a tree. He peeled and devoured it immediately. One after another, he ate. Shortly afterwards, he began feeling cramping pains in his stomach. He started puking and sweating profusely. He thought it was connected to an empty stomach combined with the excessive eating of mangos that caused the discomfort. He looked around to see if there was anyone who could help him. He noticed a house not far.

"Perhaps, the people who live there can help me," he wondered.

Holding his stomach and vomiting along the way, he finally reached the house. By now, the pain had gotten worst. He knocked on the door hoping for a generous person to come to his aid. He knocked again. This time he heard footsteps. James eyes widened when he saw the person who opened the door. In that instant the pain and discomfort were dismissed from his mind. His heart started beating faster as he took a step back.

"Welcome, my brother," the man said with a benevolent tone. It was Joseph, the man he humiliated, beat, and ejected from the land.

James quickly lowered his head and turned around to leave. He felt immense shame and remorse. Tears began rolling down his face. Joseph quickly went to him and placed his arm around his shoulders.

"The past is the past. Today is a new day. You have journeyed long. Now, it is time for you to rest. My home is your home. Let's go inside. There you will find food and shelter."

"How can you forgive me? I did you and your family so much harm," James said, in a trembling voice.

"You are my brother. Jesus forgave those who did him wrong. Who am I not to forgive? To forgive is to free oneself. Those who hold on to revenge or harsh feelings toward others cannot move forward. They remain trapped in the past. It is a time to rejoice because God has sent you here. You were lost, and now you have found your way. Come, here you will find peace," Joseph replied.

James could scarcely walk. His legs were weak and heart was beating rapidly. Joseph helped him by holding him firmly around the waist.

"Don't worry. I am here for you. It's going to be alright," Joseph assured him.

When they went inside, Joseph's wife and the children came over and greeted him. Immediately, he was taken to a room and told to rest. The children brought him food, while Joseph's wife nursed his wounds.

"How can they be so loving toward a man who beat their father and husband, and kicked them out of their house?" James wondered.

James remained in recovery for weeks. When he was strong enough to move, James got up and proceeded to get ready to leave.

"Where are you going?" Joseph asked.

"I have bothered you and your family long enough. It is time for me to leave. I will never be able to repay you. Thank you for all you and your family have done for me," James said in an emotional tone.

"There is no need for you to leave. This is also your home. Stay here and find the peace your soul is yearning for," Joseph uttered.

Joseph's wife and children had entered the room. The children embraced James and asked him to stay. "You are a part of this family. This is your home. Stay with us," Joseph's wife stated.

James lifted his head and with tears of joy said, "Thank you, God. You have shown me the true meaning of love. Love is the key to happiness. All the land and riches of the world cannot replace it."

James agreed to stay. He became a part of the family, working hard alongside Joseph. Together, they cultivated the land and shared the crops with the less fortunate. He discovered that love for other human beings was eternal; while love for material possessions was transitory.

Once a greedy and selfish man, James had converted into a humble and generous man. He was now a man of God, spreading love and compassion to all of God's children.

CHAPTER 11

LOVE THY MOTHER

God said, "Honor thy father and thy mother; that thy days may be long upon the land which the Lord thy God giveth thee." However, these words have become meaningless to many individuals. They are more into seeking self-gratification than displaying compassion to the elderly. I am well familiar with this last statement. I lived a similar experience of being neglected and treated as an outcast unworthy of love, affection, or visits by my son and grandchildren.

Nursing homes can be the loneliest place in the world when your loved ones have completely abandoned you. My son's visits were rare, and those of my grandchildren were nil. For many years, I lived a life of desolation. I felt imprisoned in my physical body. Loneliness and isolation were my everyday companions. I yearned for the simple things in life. The things we take for granted, such as a smile, a gentle touch, a word of kindness or a kiss on the forehead. Heavy tears bathed my face every minute of the day.

Each morning, one of the nursing home attendants dressed, fed, placed me in a wheelchair and pushed me to a corner of the room where a window was. The women that came to dress and feed me did so in a detached manner. They possessed expressionless and unsmiling faces. I was always left alone to stare out the window. Not even an inspiring scene was available to help distract me from the immense sorrow I felt inside. The view from the window was dismal. It was the back of another section of the nursing home. There were no windows where one could see any form of life. It was just a plain dark brick wall. If I looked up, I could see a small part of the sky, which I would stare at for long periods of time praying and asking God to take me away. I no longer wanted to live. When I wasn't looking up and praying, I was staring down at my wrinkly and frail looking hands drenched with my falling tears.

My room had become my prison cell. It was the place where I endured the torments of isolation and depression. I suffered from the greatest illness of all-the illness of heartache. The cure was an act of kindness mixed with love, which I had none.

Day after day, the routine and scene were the same. The same unfriendly and unhappy faces greeted me each morning. There were no good mornings, smiles, or stimulating conversations. On two separate occasions, I had two lovely young attendants who were pleasant. They would cheer me up, ask me how I was doing and sometimes bring me flowers. However, their stay was short. I never saw them again.

Then one day, I woke up and found myself standing in front of a lifeless body. It was the body of an old, frail woman. As I looked closely, I noticed that it was myself. At first, I was confused. "Am I dreaming?" I questioned myself. Soon reality began to settle in. It was not a dream. My terrestrial existence had ended. God had granted my wish. I was free. I no longer carried the burden of earthly emotions and/or illnesses. Feelings of depression and loneliness were lifted from me. I had released myself from a body that had become my prison. My body was no longer weak and sickly. I had reversed to my younger and healthy self. I was very much alive in a spiritual sense.

When I turned around, my parents and grandmother were standing in front of an immense bright light. They had come to take me home. They gave me a welcoming smile and guided me into the light.

It was during my healing process that I was allowed to review my recent earthly incarnated visit. My initial recollection was of a joyful time. It was a time of innocence and joy- a time where family values were priority and neighbors were always available to help each other.

It was summertime in Brooklyn, New York. Mostly, everyone was outdoors trying to enjoy the wonderful weather or escape the heat in their apartments. The children played outside, while the adults sat in front of their buildings chatting and taking pleasure in the fresh warm breeze that came every so often. When the ice cream man showed up, the kids called their parents and asked for money to buy ice cream. If our mothers were in the house, they would place money in a brown paper bag and throw it out the window. With money in our hands, my brother and I would run to the truck and purchase our favorite ice cream cones. Licking our cones, we walked back slowly enjoying our ice cream. If someone didn't have money to buy ice cream, we would share. Definitely, it was a happy time. Kids respected adults and adults looked out for the kids.

"Marie...Marie. Get your brother and come upstairs. Dinner is ready."

That was the sweet voice of my mother. She had pulled her head out the window from our third floor apartment. I stopped whatever I was doing, ran across the street to the park and fetched my brother.

"Carl, we have to go," I yelled.

"Okay, I'm coming," he replied.

I would run ahead only to be outrun by my brother who was two years older than me. He was like a passing tornado.

"You can't catch me," he would say as he ran up the stairs. Although I tried my best, I was not fast enough. When we got upstairs, my father and grandfather would be in the living room watching television waiting for dinner to be served. They had arrived earlier from work. My mother and grandmother were in the kitchen getting dinner ready.

Before running to the bathroom to wash up, we went to the living room to greet my father and grandfather. They always had a piece of chocolate candy for us. The rule was that we needed to eat dinner first before having the candy.

Dinnertime was an important event in our family. It was a time where the family bonded. We talked about everything. My father would always inquire about our day.

"How was your day?" he asked us.

"It was fine. Katy's birthday is next week and she invited me. Can I go?" I recall saying one time.

My father looked at me and smiled. "I don't see why not. Did you ask your mother for permission?" My mother always said yes.

My family, which consisted of my parents, paternal grandparents, brother, and me, was extremely close.

From time to time, my brother and I would fight over childish things. I recall having a fight with my brother over something trivial. My father walked into the room and sat us down. Then, he asked us, "Do you hate each other?"

I looked at my brother; he looked at me; and we gave each other dirty looks by rolling our eyes.

Once again, my father asked us, "Do you hate each other?"

"She started first," my brother said. Then, I repeated the same thing about him.

"You both need to understand one thing. The blood that runs in her veins is the same blood that runs in yours. We are family. We can disagree, but we should never hate each other. When one family member is hurting, it affects the rest of the family. We need to love and support each other. Without love, the family is divided. It is like a hand with missing fingers. It is incomplete. A loving and supportive family is more valuable than all the riches of the world. There is enough hate outside. Let's not bring it indoors." he told us.

My brother and I looked at each other and smiled after the sermon.

One thing about my brother and me was that we always loved, protected, and supported each other. I guess my father's sermon helped us to solidify our relationship.

In addition to my father teaching us family values, my mother taught us the value of caring for others. She would tell us, "It is our duty to help others, especially the elderly."

Ms. Jones was our next-door neighbor. She was an elderly woman who lived alone. Her husband had died some time back. A few years after her husband passed away, she fell and fractured her hipbone. She never recovered fully and had to use a cane to move around. Although she was an older woman, she was always neatly dressed with her hair elegantly combed back in a bun.

A faint scent of her favorite lily of the valley fragrance roamed the air of her apartment. It was a pleasant, sweet floral scent.

Every day, my mother would prepare a large dinner plate for Ms. Jones. My mother gave her enough for her to eat dinner and lunch the following day. It was my job to take it to her. I loved going over to her apartment. She was such an interesting person and a fascinating storyteller. In addition, she always served me ice cream and cookies. If she didn't have any, she gave me money and asked me to buy some. Each time, I received an extra quarter from her.

I would spend hours in her apartment listening to her stories about her travels around the world. She showed me pictures of her and her husband in different places. It was the first time I had seen a picture of the sphinx.

Besides her story telling, she allowed me to comb her hair. She had beautiful long white straight hair. Although I enjoyed our visits together, I felt she cherished them more. I was a companion who helped her keep her old memories alive and at the same time make new ones. I never knew if she had any relatives. I never saw anyone visiting her.

One day, I went over to take a plate of food. I knocked several times, but she never came to the door. I ran home and informed my mother. My mother rushed over to see what was wrong. Ms. Jones had given her a key in case of emergencies.

"Hello, Ms. Jones. Where are you?" my mother said.

No answer was received. When my mother walked into the bedroom, Ms. Jones was in bed with her eyes closed and a smile on her face as if having a pleasant dream. She had passed away in her sleep.

It took me a while to overcome her death. She was such a wonderful and generous person.

When I was in my early twenties, difficult times surfaced. My grandparents and father had passed away. Also, I had married, gave birth to a baby boy and divorced two years later. The father of my son had disappeared never to be seen again. The only good thing that kept me going was having my son and mother by my side. After the death of my father, my mother moved in with me. She took care of my son while I worked and took night courses in a community college. I took pride in being a good mother and daughter.

Occasionally, I took a second job. I didn't want my son or mother to lack anything. I made sure my son had more than enough. No sacrifice was too great to make for the happiness of my son. He was the love of my life. Although some people said that I spoiled him, I did not care.

I dated a few times but never re-married. I was extremely devoted to my son and did not want to disrupt our relationship.

One of the happiest days of my life was when my son graduated from college. I was thrilled when he told me that he wanted to attend a Master's program. I gave him all the financial support he needed. I wanted him to be happy and succeed in life.

After two years, he graduated with a Master's degree in finance. He quickly got a good paying job. I was the proudest mother in the entire universe. As a gift, I gave him the down payment for a co-op apartment.

Soon afterward, he met Joan. Within a year, they were married. Joan was a lovely, humble and caring girl who we adored. Before long, Joshua was born bringing enormous joy to the family.

I considered my life to be perfect. I was healthy with a good job, my mother was living with me, and my son was happily married with an adorable son. I was truly blessed.

Three years later, my mother had a stroke. I was devastated. After a stay in the hospital and rehab center, I brought her home. The people from the rehab center recommended she be placed in a nursing home because she had lost the use of her left side and was unable to speak coherently. I immediately disagreed and demanded her release. My brother and I agreed to hire a person to take care of her while I worked. He would visit frequently and spent time with her.

At night, I would feed her, read her stories, talk to her about past times and play soothing music to make her relax. Then, I would rest next to her, sing her a made up song and stroke her hair.

"Sleep, my precious Queen. Sleep and let God's angels cradle you in their divine arms until you fall into a peaceful sleep. Sleep, my precious Queen. Sleep. Remember, you are loved by all. Sleep, my precious Queen."

She would turn around, kiss me and then fall asleep.

On her birthday, my brother, his two sons, my son, Joan, the baby and I surprised her with her favorite cake. It was coconut cake with a strawberry filling. When she saw all of us together, joyful tears began rolling down her face. You could see the immense happiness on her face. There was a glow that radiated from her eyes.

"Grandma, you are the most precious person in the world. Happy birthday. I love you," one of my brother's son shouted.

She smiled and signaled him to get closer. When he did, she kissed him on his face. Soon everyone was demanding a kiss from her. It was an unforgettable moment.

Two days later, I walked into the room to kiss her good morning and noticed the same look Ms. Jones had many years ago. She had peacefully passed away in her sleep. The emotional pain I experienced was indescribable. I had lost my best friend. I remained in mourning for some time.

A year later, grueling news appeared at my doorstep. After five years, of what I thought was a happy marriage, my son informed me that he was getting a divorce. I was distraught. I loved Joan very much. She was like a daughter to me. She had been such a comfort after the passing of my mother. She would check on me, bring me groceries and spend time just listening to me. I tried to reason with him and suggested marriage counseling. However, he was resolved in his decision.

"I don't love Joan anymore and want out of the marriage," he replied.

Later, I learned that he had met a woman in his job, which was the main cause of his breakup. He quickly married her after his divorce was finalized.

His new wife was nothing like Joan. She was materialistic and self-centered. She rarely came to visit me, always complaining she was not feeling well. I was never invited to their home. They soon had three children. Whenever they needed a babysitter, my son would call and say he was dropping the kids so they could spend some time with me. Each time he dropped the children, his wife stayed in the car. By now, Joan had remarried and moved to another state. I seldom saw Joshua.

I did not mind babysitting my grandchildren. I enjoyed their company. However, I saw less of them as they got older. Whenever my son visited, which was two or three times a month, he would say that they were busy with schoolwork or other activities. There was always an excuse.

One day, I decided to have Thanksgiving dinner in my place. I wanted to gather my family together and spend some quality time with them. I invited my son, his family and my brother. My son and brother agreed to come. Everything was all set.

My brother, whose wife had passed away and sons had moved to the west coast, was planning to relocate and live with his youngest son. In addition to celebrating Thanksgiving, it was a farewell dinner for my brother.

For two days, I lovingly prepared my son's favorite dishes. I was so elated and anxious to see and spend time with my family. The table was set and the food was ready to be served. My brother arrived on time. We waited two hours for my son and his family to arrive. They did not show up. We decided to sit and eat. My brother, noticing my disappointment, said, "Don't worry. Maybe they got stuck somewhere!" Four hours later, the phone rang. It was my son.

"Hi, mom. Sorry, but we won't be going over. We stopped at some friends' house and didn't realize it was so late. The kids are tired. So, we are going home. I'll talk to you tomorrow. Good night."

I was in a state of disbelief. "How could he do this to me? He selected to have Thanksgiving dinner with friends and treat me as a stranger," I said, choking on my words and tears clouding my vision. "Was I such a horrible mother?" I asked my brother.

"You were the best mother to your son. You gave him everything. Don't cry," he said. My brother tried to console me, but the pain was too great.

He decided to stay overnight and keep me company. The next day, I gave him food for a few days and some for two of his neighbors that I knew very well.

"Are you alright?" he asked.

"It hurts, but I will survive. For some reason, his wife does not like me and is trying to keep my son away from me. I guess she sees me as a threat. I will leave it in God's hands. Don't worry. I am fine."

A few days later, my son called.

"Hi, sorry about the other day,"

"It's okay. I had a wonderful time with Carl. We reminisced about the past when we were kids and how family values were so important to us," I said.

There was a brief pause and then he spoke.

"Okay. I have to go now. Speak to you soon."

When I was 75 years old, I fell and broke my hipbone. I was hospitalized and had a hip replacement. During my stay in the hospital and rehab, I received visits from friends but none from my grandchildren. By this time, my brother, who had relocated to the west coast, had passed away.

The day of my discharge from rehab, my son picked me up. He began talking about nursing homes, and the many benefits they provided. When I refused adamantly to entertain his suggestion, the conversation was terminated.

During my recovery period, I had a visiting nurse and home attendant. They were so sweet and loving. Once a month, my son would visit me. His visits became quite annoying. His main topic was nursing homes. He appeared to be obsessed with erroneous thoughts of me being an invalid. Every time, the topic was presented, an argument would immediately ensue, causing him to storm out the door.

As for my grandchildren, they never came to visit me. No, I'm wrong. One of my grandsons did come over to ask for money. When I gave him ten dollars, he vanished quickly without saying thank you or goodbye.

Two years later, I was back in the hospital. I had fallen and fractured my other hip. After a medical procedure and a short hospital stay, I was placed in a rehabilitation center. I stayed several weeks. My son only came to visit me three or four times during my entire stay. As for my grandchildren, they never showed up. My neighbors and friends were the ones who visited me faithfully, made me laugh and gave me love.

I returned home to discover that my days were numbered. When I was in the hospital, my son insisted that I give him power of attorney. After much thought, I gave in. I never thought he would use it against me. Behind my back, arrangements were made to place me in a nursing home. His reason was that I was getting too old to take care of myself. How would he know? He was never around to see that I was never alone. I had my neighbors, friends and a terrific home attendant.

Too sick and tired, I eventually gave in without a fight. All of my precious belongings were dispersed, and I was shipped away to a nursing home. That was the most disheartening day of my life. I felt like an unwanted human being placed in the middle of nowhere to die alone. Even though I was wheelchair bound, my mind was lucid.

Initially, a few friends came to visit me but soon the visits stopped. The traveling was too much for them. I was in a nursing home far from where I lived.

At first, my son would visit two or three times a month staying for just a few minutes. Later, the visits were cut down to once a month, and eventually to rare occasions.

"Do you need something? I need to go. I have something I need to do," he would say. This was his speech every time he visited. Never once did he express any affection or ask me how I was feeling.

One day, he came to visit and as usual repeated his same performance. "Do you need something? I need to go. Aida is waiting for me in the car. I need to drop her off at the beauty salon," he said.

"Why didn't she come up to see me?" I asked.

"She hates hospitals and nursing homes. She says they are so depressing."

"Do your children feel the same way?"

"Oh mom, please stop acting like the victim. We all have active lives. We can't stop everything to run here and entertain you. Mom, I have to go now," he said a bit agitated.

Although I lacked family love, I found much comfort in a new friend. Her name was Betty. She became my best friend. She came to the nursing home three months after me. We hit it off immediately. Her situation was similar to mine. We were the abandoned parents of ungrateful children.

Betty had three children-two daughters and a son. On rare occasions, her oldest daughter dropped by for a quick visit. I never saw the other two. Whenever, I did not see her, I knew she was experiencing a depressed moment. I immediately rolled my wheelchair and dropped by her room that was adjacent to mine. She would be sitting near the edge of the bed with tears in her eyes staring at photos of her children and grandchildren.

"I am so alone. No one cares for me. I gave so much to my children and grandchildren, and they can't take a moment to visit me. I am old and expendable. They don't need me anymore," she said weeping while rocking back and forth.

I grabbed her hands and cried. I knew very well the pain she was experiencing.

Holidays were the worst time for us. None of our relatives came to visit us. Betty and I would hug each other and cry. Then, I would smile and say, "At least we have each other." That statement always made her feel better.

After two years, Betty's health began to decline. She was in and out of hospitals. Then, one day, Betty passed away in her sleep. My life was never the same after that. My only friend had gone away, leaving me behind.

With Betty gone, my life was empty. I had no friends or family.

The majority of the patients were either seriously ill or in a catatonic state. Days turned into weeks, weeks turned into months, and months turned into years. Nothing changed in my life. As mentioned in the beginning, loneliness and isolation were my only companions. It was when I detached from my physical body that I began to live.

After the healing process, I was allowed to visit my terrestrial family on Earth. My son was much older and facing the same loneliness that I experienced. He lost almost everything in a nasty divorce battle. He had retired and lived in a small apartment by himself. His children rarely called or visited. He spends days and weeks in his apartment alone. He seemed to be forgotten by all.

At times, he would call out my name. He even asked God to forgive him for all his misdeeds. Often, with tears rolling down his face, he prayed.

"Oh, dear God, forgive me. You gave me a wonderful mother who gave me everything, and I did not appreciate or value her. When she needed me, I showed her no love or compassion. I was selfish. Now, she is gone, and I am feeling the weight of my sins. She did so much for me; and I did very little for her. She was the only person who loved me unconditionally. What a fool I was. You gave me a precious gem that I never valued. Please, have mercy on my soul. Mother, if you are around and can hear me, please forgive me for my lack of compassion and love."

Upon hearing his plead, I would whisper in his ear, "I forgive you because I never stopped loving you. For you are my son."

CHAPTER 12

MESSAGE FROM GOD

Excuse me. Can I have a few minutes of your time? I want to know why you have blocked me from your heart and life. What have I done for you to distant yourself from me? Why do you constantly reject my love and continue to hurt me? Have I not been a good Father?

When you were dehydrated, I gave you water to quench your thirst; when you were starving, I provided food to alleviate your hunger; when you were cold, I clothed you and kept you warm; and when you lacked a place to rest, I gave you refuge. I bestowed upon you my commandments so that you could follow the correct path. I even sent my beloved son to show you the way. Instead of being appreciative, you were never satisfied and wanted more. Nevertheless, I continued to love you.

In the beginning of time, you stood in the light sharing your thoughts and dreams with me. You often spoke my name with much love and admiration. Whenever a meaningful or insignificant event occurred in your life, you were quick to share the news with me. We were inseparable.

However, as time progressed, you began moving away from the light and hiding behind the shadows. Slowly, you severed the ties between us. There was less sharing and bonding.

Even though numerous times you went astray and hurt me profoundly, I stood by your side waiting for you to come to your senses. I never deserted you. I am a forgiving and compassionate Father whose love for you is eternal.

Now, you defiantly ignore me. You have banished me from your life. Days, weeks and months go by without my name being uttered. Whenever I hear my name mentioned, it's either to ask me for materialistic wants or blame me for some mishap in your life. Yet, when you turned your back on me and blamed me for all your personal misfortunes, I remained by your side and continued to love you.

Since I am not a God of money or material riches, I have become obsolete and meaningless in your life.

On countless occasions, I have sent my emissaries to inform you of my love and disappointments. Their mission was not only to inform you, but also to guide you onto the right direction. However, many continued to drift on the path of darkness and uncertainties. What else can a father do?

In an effort to set you free to make personal choices, I gave you the gift of free will. Yet, when something is amiss in your life, you are prompt to blame me. I presume it is easier to accuse me than to accept responsibility for your actions. Every choice has an outcome. Although several see me as a cruel God, I continue to shower you with love.

It is heartbreaking to know that you don't have any time for me. You spend lots of time working out in the gym or socializing with friends, but can't take a second to lift your head and say hello. Am I so undeserving of your time and love?

In recent times, the energy of darkness has seized the souls of many.

Countless individuals around the globe have acquired a passion for violence, relishing the suffering and pain of others. How quickly you have disregarded one of my precious commandments: thy shall not kill. But, since I don't exist in your life, you don't care about my commandments or me.

Presently, a powerful sinister force is manipulating you. It is keeping you busy while your soul is being entangled in a web of darkness and isolation. Electronic gadgets are being used to control you. As your obsession with texting, taking selfies, chatting on social media and surfing the internet increases, your soul will commence to weaken. As the soul begins to decline, it will gradually descend into a black void.

I find it amusing as well as sad that you feel yourself completely lost without these devices, but not a bit concerned about whether or not I am walking by your side. Even though you have forgotten me, I have not abandoned you.

There was a time when my name was cited every morning in schools. Then, one day, the practice disappeared. My name was just a memory. I guess the school system saw me as being unworthy.

Some people call themselves atheists. They deny my existence and discredit my work in every possible way. It's okay. I love you all the same whether you have faith in me or not.

Others speak my name only to manipulate individuals into doing wrongful deeds. They spread hate and falsehoods. They preach, "God wants us to eliminate the infidels...In the name of God you will burn and go to hell...God doesn't like gays...God doesn't like blacks...God doesn't like Jews...God has given us the authority to kill...God only recognizes our religion as the true religion...It is God's will." These declarations as well as others have nothing to do with me. They are fabrications created by man to gain control of the minds of humans and generate hostility and hatred among my children.

Then, you have others who mention my name only to accuse me of causing all the havoc that the world is presently facing. They regard me as a God of vengeance and hate. What happened to free will? The present situation of this planet is the result of your choices. Remember, each choice has an outcome.

Why would I want to eradicate humanity and the planet I so lovingly created? I have shown you immense love. Instead of emulating and practicing it, you prefer to hate and destroy. Each time I see my children turning against each other it offends me deeply. I am not a God of vengeance or hate. I am a God of mercy and love.

I created Earth for the enjoyment of all my children. Moreover, I gave you free will in hope you would make correct choices. I wanted my children to work collectively to enrich and embellish the land. Instead, your greed has led you to divide, destroy, pillage, and pollute the land. Your materialistic cravings and malicious ambition have shattered the unity of humanity. You are slowly devouring the planet.

Your choices have created a chaotic world in which you are being held hostage. It is up to you to release yourself by unlocking the door to your cell. Let me help you to liberate yourself and accomplish a better loving situation. I am here for you.

A disease called apathy has infected Earth. The fabric of humanity is being torn apart. The legend of Cain and Abel is being repeated continuously. The suffering of others is inconsequential. People roam the streets of your cities sending text messages, talking on their cell phones, or listening to music on their iPods while ignoring the misery and pain of those around them. Few take the time to stop and offer the homeless something to eat. Some view these less fortunate individuals as outcasts or a disease that should be eliminated from the planet. The foundations of many families are crumbling. Children are abandoning their elderly parents. And, in certain cases, parents are forgetting their parental obligations. Depraved acts, such as killings, assaults, abuse, neglect and so on, are being committed every day without any remorse. My children have lost all sense of direction or purpose. Their hearts are hollow while their souls are lingering in an abyss of darkness. Anger and indifference infuse the air. How can anyone think this is of my doing? You need to wake up. You are lost in a labyrinth. Let me help you.

In the past, there have been individuals who have implanted hate in the hearts and minds of my children. They have used my name to wage war and wreak havoc. They control and manipulate others as if they were puppets on a string. However, the present situation is far greater and more dangerous. Massive destructive weapons are being built that can eliminate the existence of humanity forever.

The economy of powerful countries is collapsing; global disasters are occurring more frequently; many countries lack food and medicine; the rich wants more while the poor gets less; and killings of innocents have skyrocketed. Still, many are doing nothing to alter the course of things except blame me for all the on-going calamities.

It saddens me to see how you are slowly eliminating each other, and refusing to comprehend and accept my simple doctrine of love. You have created a world that lacks love, compassion, and understanding.

Once again, wake up before it is too late. Liberate yourself from the negativity that roams the planet. Unlock the chains that are keeping you captive. Open up your heart and let me in. Let me fill it with love and compassion.

My foremost wish is for my children to love and respect each other. Also, to work together and make the planet a better place for all. Don't block me out of your life. Let me help you and show you the way.

Come and embrace me. I have been waiting patiently for you. Let us celebrate your return. I am the Father who has loved you from the beginning of time and will continue to love you to the end.

God said, "Let there be Love." And, Love began pouring onto the Earth. All we need to do is open up our hearts and let it in. Let us spread God's love and love one another. Blessings to all.

ABOUT THE AUTHOR

The author is a native New Yorker of Puerto Rican descent. She has a master's degree in psychological counseling from Columbia University and is a graduate from the Alfred Adler Institute. In addition, she possesses a master's degree from the Tri-State College of Acupuncture.

She was raised to believe in Spiritism and continues to practice many of its ideologies. Additionally, she has traveled to various parts of the world exploring the spiritual practices of diverse religions.

She has written another book-My Spiritual Journey.

Made in the USA
Middletown, DE
09 March 2017